DICK SPRING
A Safe Pair of Hands!

Tim Ryan

BLACKWATER PRESS

Printed in Ireland at the press of the publishers

© Blackwater Press, 1993
Broomhill Business Park,
Broomhill Road,
Tallaght,
Dublin 24

ISBN 0 86121 493 5

Cover Design
Philip Ryan

Contents

Acknowledgements

This book was written without the co-operation of Dick Spring. This was of his choosing.

I would like to thank sincerely those who kindly spoke to me of their association with Dick Spring, in the world of sport, politics and his home constituency. Their names appear throughout the following pages.

I wish to acknowledge also the assistance of the library and photographic departments of *The Irish Press, The Irish Times, The Kerryman, The Nenagh Guardian,* as well as Tralee Public Library and the National Library.

A special word of thanks to Michael O'Sullivan for allowing me access to the unpublished manuscript of *Mary Robinson: The Life and Times of an Irish Liberal.*

Thanks, too, to Frank Quilter, John Moran, Jerry Scanlan, Eamonn Farrell and Kevin Coleman.

Finally, my thanks to John O'Connor of Blackwater Press for his constant encouragement and to Anna O'Donovan for bringing it all together.

Foreword

Saturday, February 3, 1979. The venue, Cardiff Arms Park.

Young Kerry barrister Dick Spring, who had recently returned home from the United States, was enjoying his second rugby cap for Ireland against an unsure Wales side.

The Irish were ahead and doing well when suddenly disaster struck for the boys in green. The ball was kicked towards the Irish line. Full-back Spring misjudged the flight and failed to catch it. Instead the ball went to Welsh forward Alan Martin who scored a magnificent try which put the reds on the road to victory.

Spring was furious with himself. He knew that whatever lay in store for him in the future, he would always be remembered for this gaffe. And it was to be so.

As late as November 1992 while canvassing for the Labour Party in the general election, it was thrown at him by a youth in Donegal.

And again at the party's annual conference in Waterford in the spring of 1993, party chairman Jim Kemmy threw it at him as he was about to deliver his Presidential address.

Kemmy touched a raw nerve and Spring snapped back that he had yet to meet somebody who had played hurling and football for his county, and rugby for his country.

Spring's spirited reply showed that he had come a long way since that fateful day in Wales in 1979.

Apart from an impressive sporting career, Dick Spring had in the meantime taken charge of a demoralised Labour Party and built it into a major political force in the Republic.

He was also enjoying his second term as Tánaiste, the prestigious number two position in the Irish Government.

A surprise choice to lead the Labour Party at the age of 32, he had taken on the mantle of Government just weeks after being elected Party Leader in 1982.

While following in the footsteps of his father, the late Dan Spring, the young Tralee man was about to cut a new path for the Labour Party which, although the oldest political party in the State, had failed to gain popular support with the electorate.

Spring was to change all this, culminating in a spectacular win of 33 Dáil seats in November 1992 which, with dismal performances by Fianna Fáil and Fine Gael, made him the power-broker.

But in doing so he had dramatically transformed the party. In many ways it is today scarcely recognisable as the party founded by James Connolly and Jim Larkin in 1912. Gone is the old rule book, the old socialism and even the starry plough. They have been replaced by a smart, attractive red rose and a new constitution.

To cater for a post-Soviet Ireland, Spring jettisoned the embarrassing bits and replaced them with broad aspirations which might equally apply to any other centre party.

But the formula worked.

Spring could have radically re-shaped the Labour Party in the right-wing mould made fashionable by Margaret Thatcher in the 1980s, but he successfully tapped the Irish mood of the 1990s. This success was seen in the voting boxes of the general election in 1992 when large numbers of wealthy and traditionally right-wing residents of Dublin 4 and Galway's fashionable Barna District gave their number one to Labour.

Now as Tánaiste in the new Fianna Fáil/Labour partnership Government, Spring demanded and was given the Foreign Affairs portfolio by Taoiseach Albert Reynolds. He is determined to resolve the centuries-old Northern Ireland question. Although he is willing to explore new initiatives, he has already lost the confidence of the Unionist parties. It is still early days, but there is every danger that

Spring could again fumble the ball.

Behind this public mask is the man Spring, a person few people know well. Those who are in his confidence say the inner-Spring is very different to the cold, aloof image he portrays in the media. He is, they say, humorous and witty.

But he does, on occasion, lose his temper in public. Members of the media, in particular, test his patience, and he has lashed out at them more than once.

Dick Spring has caught the popular imagination. In many ways he represents the modern-day Ireland of the 1990s. Already he has joined the ranks of the other important political figures of this century – de Valera, Lemass, Lynch and FitzGerald.

Aged only 43, his impact on Irish life has been remarkable, but the full story has not been told until now.

1

THE HOME TEAM

One evening in 1943 a young psychiatric nurse in St Finian's Hospital in Killarney, Co Kerry, Anna Laide, set off to cycle the 31-mile journey from Killarney to Kilflynn.

Her boyfriend, a young trade union official named Dan Spring, was contesting the general election for the Labour Party for the first time, and she was determined to give him her number one vote.

Anna's mission was complicated by the fact that she could not tell her father about it. The romance of the occasion was lost on him, and he had expected the whole family to turn out and vote for the farmers' candidate in the election.

"She told her mother, but she couldn't break it to her dad that she wouldn't be voting for Paddy Finnucane that day," her son Arthur recalled.

Dan Spring used to see her cycling home from her job. These days she laughs when she remembers him saying he married her to take her down off the bike.

Politics interfered with the couple's wedding plans, which were set for the first week in June 1944. However, an election was called on May 28 and Dan, who had been a TD only since the previous year, had to take to the hustings.

"I received a phone call that day from his brother Frank in Tralee, who told me the campaign was getting under way immediately," she later recalled. "I met Dan at Killarney railway station on his way back from Dublin.

"We had to call off the wedding, but I had always wanted to

be a June bride. We were married at 6am on 29 June in St John's Church, Tralee."

Dan Spring had been born in Tralee in July 1910. An all-round young man, he had developed a keen interest in sport while he worked as a labourer in a flour milling firm in Tralee.

At the age of 22 he was a substitute on the Kerry football team which won the 1932 All-Ireland, and played for Kerry's winning teams in 1939 and 1940 (he captained the 1940 side).

It was his experience while working in the harsh economic climate of the 1930s and early 1940s that inspired him to take up the cause of his fellow workers. This eventually led him to become the secretary of the local ITGWU branch. Gradually, he moved into local and national politics.

In 1923, Kerry was just one Dáil constituency with seven seats. This continued until 1935 when it was divided into North and South. North Kerry returned four members to Leinster House and South Kerry three.

Dan Spring faced considerable odds in 1943 when he stood for election but managed to give the Labour Party its first seat in the county with 5,155 first preference votes. The farmers' candidate, Paddy Finnucane, was also elected, thereby depriving Fianna Fáil and Fine Gael of a seat each. He increased his vote in the general election the following year to 8,429 first preference votes, but was back again to 5,877 in 1948. He survived as a deputy with unbroken service until 1981, but the period was not without its high drama.

In 1956, Dan Spring was appointed Parliamentary Secretary (equivalent to Minister of State) to the Minister for Local Government in the second Coalition Government. However, his vote did not increase and he came under severe electoral pressure when the number of seats in North Kerry was reduced to three in 1961 following a constituency revision. He received his lowest vote ever in the 1969 general election, 4,913 first preference votes, but survived.

Kerry is arguably one of the most Republican counties in the country, and Dan Spring was acutely aware of this tradition.

When scarcely a year in the Dáil, both Dan Spring and Paddy Finnucane were expelled from the House on 30 November 1944, for trying to stop the execution of IRA chief-of-staff, Charlie Kerins, who was convicted of shooting a Garda detective. Kerins had been a friend and a next-door neighbour of the Springs in his youth. The efforts failed, and Kerins was hanged on the morning of 1 December.

During the 1950s, Kerry North returned a Clann na Poblachta deputy while the South elected an abstentionist Sinn Féiner. By contrast, during the 35 years Dan Spring was a Dáil deputy, Fine Gael was not represented for 17 of those years.

In his book, *The Irish Labour Party in Transition 1957-1982*, Michael Gallagher argues that a more Republican attitude among TDs from rural constituencies – especially those in the south-west, such as Kerry, Limerick and Tipperary, represented by Spring, Stevie Coughlan and Seán Treacy – could be attributed "either to a direct relationship between ignorance and distance from the Border, or to the traditionally Republican nature of these constituencies, which were the strongholds of the IRA in 1918-21 period and of the anti-Treatyites during the Civil War".

Spring's ability to capture the Republican vote is shown by the fact that in the 1973 general election when Kevin Boland's Aontacht Éireann party fielded a strong candidate, Joe Keohane, a household name in GAA circles, he made little impact and only managed to win 695 votes. Half of them were transferred back to Dan Spring.

Four years later, in 1977, the first count appeared to indicate that the end had at last arrived. A massive anti-Coalition swing had assured Fianna Fáil of two of the three seats, while Dan Spring trailed 2,000 votes behind Fine Gael in the contest for the final seat.

Yet, as the count progressed, Spring somehow managed to overcome his hapless rival, Gerard Lynch, and finally won out by a margin of just 307 votes. Exactly ten years later, his son was to have his closest electoral shave ever when he would hang on by a margin of just four votes.

How Dan Spring managed to survive as a Dáil deputy against all the odds is a tribute to his political astuteness – and the ever-present assistance of his wife, Anna.

Apart from his brief period as a Parliamentary Secretary in 1956-57, his term in the Dáil was undistinguished as a back-bencher, very much in keeping with the tradition of mostly silent Kerry deputies.

"Dan Spring is an extraordinary political survivor, a throwback to a bygone age," said an article in an issue of *Hibernia* in 1979. "A massive Skellig of a man, he stands isolated from the mainland of contemporary politics, oblivious to the storms and currents swirling about him. By all conventional logic he should long since have faded from the Dáil scene together with Labour contemporaries such as Paddy Tierney and Paddy McAuliffe. Yet, like that ageless Kerryman, Fianna Fáil's Chubb O'Connor, he continues to confound the pundits who constantly and inaccurately forecast his demise."

Dan Spring enjoyed a number of advantages – sound record of constituency service, the ITGWU connection and, of course, the All-Ireland football medals. Over the years, he symbolised the steadfast, rural TD, conservative and cautious in most matters, a good worker, but a rare contributor to Dáil debates. He once remarked wryly that he had seen too many people talking their way into the Oireachtas, only then to turn around and talk their way out again!

When Labour moved decisively to the Left in the late 1960s, and recruited a number of prominent intellectuals, notably Dr Conor Cruise-O'Brien and Justin Keating, he clearly distanced himself from the party's new image in his own constituency.

Geography also played its part.

In his later years as a Dáil deputy, Dan Spring's main rivals were Fine Gael's Gerard Lynch and Fianna Fáil's Kit Aherne, both of whom lived at the northern end of the constituency, in Listowel and Ballybunion respectively.

Meanwhile, Dan Spring monopolised Tralee. While the other parties went through the motions of fielding Tralee-based candidates, a high percentage of their votes would inevitably transfer back to Spring, much to their annoyance. For example, in the 1977 general election, he won back 1,800 transfers from Fianna Fáil, and this at the end of a Coalition period between Fine Gael and Labour!

But there was also the Spring element of political shrewdness and cunning.

In 1969 the Labour Party Administrative Council, in a rush of blood to the head that caused many candidates to lose their deposits, decided that all sitting deputies should take on a running mate for the campaign.

Spring ignored the order, which was given to him personally by Party General Secretary, Brendan Halligan, and joined with Cork South-West Deputy Michael Pat Murphy in running alone. Three other Munster deputies, Tom Kyne, Eileen Desmond and Paddy McAuliffe obeyed the instruction, split the Labour vote and lost their seats by 101, 320 and 419 votes respectively.

Anna Spring was central to the move to defy headquarters. Following what one newspaper described as a "bit of hugger mugger between Dan, Anna and a few others", it was announced that Anna would be the second candidate. The Administrative Council knew well that she would withdraw within 24 hours of the closing of nominations and just gave up in sheer frustration!

In his election literature Dan Spring did not mention the Labour Party at all. It simply stated that he had worked for the constituency for 26 years and urged: "He helps you, now you help him."

The *Kerryman* newspaper observed at the time that Spring's personalised campaign was a far cry from Labour's "New Republic", but it was nevertheless "the very stuff of politics in Co Kerry and is likely to see him re-elected".

While Labour was routed in the rest of Munster, his strategy proved to be correct and he held his seat.

A few years later, Dan Spring again teamed up with Michael Pat Murphy and Limerick's Stevie Coughlan in defying the party on the contraception issue. Such bursts of independence probably did him no harm at all at election time.

Dan Spring's loyalty to and respect for the controversial deputy, Stevie Coughlan, was shown by the fact that he was the only rural deputy to vote against the removal of the whip from him at the 1972 Annual Conference (the others were John O'Connell and Michael D Higgins).

Like Michael Pat Murphy in Cork South-West, Seán Treacy in Tipperary South, or John Ryan in Tipperary North, Dan Spring ran a political machine in North Kerry. His vote reflected the force of his personality as much as anything else. While he was very committed to the Labour Party and trade union principles, he was capable of plucking votes from all shades of political opinion, right across the political spectrum. He had, of course, his own individual views on how things should be done.

In his book *Labour – The Price of Power* former Labour deputy, John Horgan, recalls that during the 1977-81 Dáil there was an occasion at a meeting of the Parliamentary Party when the

Assistant General Secretary, Séamus Scally, read out the standing of various Members in relation to their monthly subscriptions to headquarters. A number of deputies were in arrears, but for relatively small amounts of money. The list was in alphabetical order and Dan Spring's name was the last to be read out. His arrears were in hundreds of pounds. According to Horgan, Spring had refused to pay the levy on some point of principle.

Spring was not present at the meeting, but a hushed silence fell over the room following the revelation. Suddenly from the back of the room the voice of Frank Cluskey could be heard to pronounce in his Dublin accent: "Spring, having exceeded the quota, is deemed elected...!"

During all of Dan Spring's Dáil years the role of his wife, Anna, should never be underestimated. She took the job as seriously as he did, working night and day to protect his Dáil seat. A tireless worker to this day, she was her husband's unpaid political secretary, his constant presence in the constituency while he was away on Dáil business. Times were often tough for the close couple, who provided well for each of their three sons and three daughters.

"The seat was never an easy one to hold because we always had the major parties to contend with," she remembered. "The seat was our bread and butter. We fought and won 11 elections and enjoyed them all."

Dan Spring died in 1988.

It is not for nothing that Anna Spring is known as "The Godmother" in North Kerry politics and she is said to "reason with" any Labour politicians who get too big for their boots in her son's constituency.

"Let's put it this way," says one party member who fell foul of her, "if anyone puts his head above the parapet, she'll shoot it off and then cut the feet from under him."

Fine Gael deputy for North Kerry, Jimmy Deenihan, describes Anna Spring as a very strong matriarchal figure. In political terms he places her in the same role as Rose Kennedy, mother of John F Kennedy, or Sinéad Bean de Valera.

"She is very competitive at election time. She doesn't recognise anyone who poses a threat to Dick or her family. In 1987 she blamed us for Dick's close shave and some felt that wrath afterwards. She sees herself as the Mother figure, as tough as you could meet in politics and somebody to be reckoned with. She has been so consistent in protecting her family over the years that people have grown to respect her – out of sheer fear in some cases! She is certainly the most powerful political woman in Kerry," says Deenihan.

Her son Arthur attributed her strengths to her unfailing instinct, rather than any academic political knowledge, a fierce protectiveness towards her family, and a real genius for organisation.

"She's still very actively involved in politics around election time, but she just doesn't stop at politics. She works for the Mental Health Association and she's trying to raise funds for the Kidney Donor Association. She has a very sound knowledge of politics – now she wouldn't be *au fait* with devaluation or anything like that – but she's very good on personalities. And, of course, Dick listens to her ......he has to!"

Dick Spring once recalled that the late David Thornley had described his mother as the Party's "stage manager".

During the November 1992 general election, Anna Spring, then a sprightly 74-year-old, arrived each morning at election head-quarters at 10am and took up duty at a long table.

Donal Hickey, the Kerry-based reporter with the *Cork Examiner,* watched her:

"She sits by a phone which rings constantly, jots down messages, gives directions to party workers and ensures that an ample supply of posters and literature is circulated to each of Labour's 30 branches in Kerry North.

"Also within arm's reach are copies of the register of electors – of which she has an encyclopaedic knowledge – and these will be sent to personating officers at every polling booth."

Anna Spring is also full of praise for her American daughter-in-law, Kristi. "She's as good a partner to Dick as I was to Dan," she said.

2

THE SEVENTIES WILL BE SOCIALIST

By the end of 1982 the Labour Party was in poor shape. Still reeling from the effects of the 1973-77 Coalition Government, and torn apart by the whole issue of Coalition, the party suddenly found itself without a leader, directly in the run-up to a general election.

Established in Clonmel in 1912 by the Irish Trade Union Congress on the principle of independent Labour representation, the party was finally launched on 1 June 1914.

"Today we see the birth of an Irish Labour Party in which there would be no room for the old lines of cleavage: no sectional politics, no disagreements, no misunderstandings; cemented by their common needs, a working-class party," declared one of the party's founders, Jim Larkin.

Much of Larkin's prophecy was to prove false.

The national struggle for independence meant that the Labour Party failed to catch the support of the working classes immediately and become a major political party. This difficulty was compounded by the fact that the party did not contest either the 1918 or 1921 general elections.

When James Connolly was executed after the 1916 Rising, the trade union leaders decided not to contest the elections for fear of alienating Northern Protestant members of the movement.

The party did, however, contest the 1922 general election and won 17 seats. The party accepted the Treaty and all but one entered the Dáil, led by Tom Johnson.

Significantly, Johnson, who was born in Liverpool, never condemned the execution of James Connolly and failed to reconcile the nationalist and socialist ideologies.

The Labour Party got off to a bad start in 1923 due to a bitter row within the ITGWU involving Jim Larkin. He fielded four candidates and all were defeated. However, the split hit Labour badly and its representation in the Dáil was reduced from 17 to 14 at a time when the number of Dáil seats had been increased from 123 to 157.

In 1927 Johnson proposed a vote of no confidence in the Government when Fianna Fáil finally entered the House but was defeated.

In the June election of that year – there was a second election in September – Labour won 22 seats, a successful figure which was equalled only in 1965, and surpassed in November 1992.

However, in August of the same year the party combined unsuccessfully with Fianna Fáil and the National League to try to oust the Cosgrave Government and replace it with a Labour/National League Coalition.

But in one of the most bizarre political incidents ever, a clever plan by Independent TD, Bryan Cooper, resulted in one Redmondite, Alderman John Jinks, who was to have voted against the Government, being sent off on the Sligo train. Cooper had plied Jinks with drink in Buswell's Hotel before calling a taxi and sending him on his way to Sligo. The Government survived on the casting vote of the Ceann Comhairle, Michael Hayes.

Tom Johnson lost his Dublin County seat in the second general election in 1927 when Cumann na nGaedhael won four seats in the constituency. His downfall was aided by a decision by Jim Larkin Jnr to contest the seat. Jim Larkin Snr actually won a seat in Dublin North but was prevented from taking it because he was bankrupt as a result of two libel actions.

Tom Johnson was replaced as leader of the Labour party by TJ O'Connell. A native of Bekan, Co Mayo, TJ O'Connell was a national school teacher before he was was appointed General Secretary of the Irish National Teachers' Organisation.

He was elected to the Dáil for Galway in 1922 and for South Mayo in 1927. He was leader of the Labour Party until 1932 when he was defeated in the election of that year. He was later elected to the Seanad and remained a Member of the Upper House until 1957.

In 1932 William Norton succeeded TJ O'Connell and remained at the helm until 1960. This period saw many changes.

Norton had first been elected to the Dáil in a by-election for Dublin County in 1926. He did not contest the June or September elections in order to ensure the success of the then Leader, Tom Johnson. William Norton was elected for the constituency of Kildare in 1932 and 1933, and later for Carlow-Kilkenny.

The party's first initiative was to support the minority Fianna Fáil Party and to take a more Republican stance. In 1940 clerical pressure caused it to remove its objective of a Workers' Republic from its Constitution.

"Big Jim" Larkin re-joined the Labour Party in 1941 and was elected to the Dáil in 1943. However, his return caused the ITGWU to disaffiliate from the Labour Party and five of the eight deputies departed to form the National Labour Party which claimed the original Labour Party was "communist dominated". North Kerry Deputy, Dan Spring, was one of the eight who joined National Labour.

Both sections of the Labour Party re-united only when they came together in the 1948-51 Coalition (Jim Larkin had died in 1947).

William Norton served as Tánaiste and Minister for Social Welfare under Taoiseach John A Costello, who was a compromise choice to lead the Government instead of the Fine Gael leader, Richard Mulcahy. It was this Government which declared the Republic in 1949.

William Norton again served as Tánaiste in the second Coalition Government from 1954 to 1957, this time as Minister for Industry and Commerce. In 1956 Dan Spring was appointed Parliamentary Secretary to the Minister for Education.

The severe financial measures adopted by Gerard Sweetman, the Minister for Finance in this Government, eventually caused its collapse. It also left a legacy for the Labour Party, which remained out of office for the next 13 years.

William Norton retired in 1960 and was replaced by Brendan Corish. Corish, who was 42 when he took over the reins of the Labour Party, was a native of Wexford and had succeeded his father, Richard, who had represented the county in the Dáil from 1922 to 1945. A Sinn Féin supporter during the War of Independence – he had been deported for a time in 1920 by the British authorities – Richard Corish had first been elected to Dáil Éireann for that party in 1921, although he did not take his seat.

Brendan Corish was elected in the by-election caused by the death of his father. During the first Coalition Government of 1948-51 he served as Parliamentary Secretary to the Minister for Local Government, and to the Minister for Defence in the 1954-57 Coalition.

Corish was determined to rebuild the Labour Party and to keep it out of Coalition for the foreseeable future. In a famous speech in Co Offaly during the 1961 general election he stated that the party would never again enter Coalition with Fine Gael. He repeated this commitment prior to the 1965 general election when the party made substantial gains, increasing its representation to 22 seats, a number it had not held since the June election of 1927.

Throughout the 1960s the Labour Party began to move distinctly to the Left and to reflect the growing militancy of industrial workers. New, young members poured into its ranks.

Intellectuals and media personalities such as Conor Cruise-O'Brien and Justin Keating joined up.

Corish was universally liked in the Labour Party. In his book, *Labour: The Price of Power,* John Horgan points out that any group of activists within the party who tried to lay blame for any disaster on his shoulders was rapidly reduced to the status of a small and querulous minority.

At the Labour Party conference in 1969, Corish told the delegates that "the Seventies will be Socialist", and that if the party at any time in the future decided to go into Coalition, he would loyally accept such a decision, but would himself retire to the back benches.

The proposer of the anti-Coalition motion was a young Cork man, Michael O'Leary, who some years later would himself become Tánaiste in a Fine Gael-led Government. However, strange and unexpected moves were taking place at the same time within the ranks of Fine Gael.

In his autobiography, *All In a Life,* the former Taoiseach, Dr Garret FitzGerald, recalls a crucial meeting of Fine Gael's Front Bench on 3 January 1968, which went on from 11am until 5pm. During the meeting, Deputy Mark Clinton proposed a merger with the Labour Party, a notion that had been gaining support in certain circles in both parties. There was general acceptance of the idea that talks should be started.

The Fine Gael leader, Liam Cosgrave, raised the issue later that week with Brendan Corish, who sought the proposal in writing. Corish was cool about the idea, fearing that news of any discussions would leak out to the media.

However, he put the idea to the Labour Party's Front Bench but reported back, saying "nothing doing", adding that he hoped there would be no more approaches from Fine Gael.

"And so," wrote Dr FitzGerald, "Fine Gael and Labour went

their separate paths as parties, although they have served in Coalitions together on three subsequent occasions. Had this move succeeded, the political history of the succeeding years would surely have been very different."

The general euphoria surrounding the Labour Party was shown by the fact that it put up 99 candidates in the 1969 general election. Spokespersons frequently talked of a breakthrough for Labour which would yield around 40 Dáil seats. However, the result was disappointing, with the loss of four seats overall from its 1965 level. The party retreated from its previous stance and, in 1970, voted to re-think the Coalition issue. This was all the more significant in that it removed the power to make a decision about entering a Coalition Government from the party conference and placed it in the hands of the Leader and the Parliamentary Party. Corish softened the blow, however, by pointing out that the Parliamentary Party would "act in consultation with the Administrative Council".

John Horgan emphasises the skill of Brendan Corish in keeping the party together during this difficult time as follows:

"It is difficult to think of any other leader who could have survived the spectacular reversal of party policy on Coalition in 1970, or who could have taken office in a Coalition Government after having promised to support Coalition only from the backbenches. In Corish's Labour party this provoked grumbles and, indeed, opposition. In the same party led by anyone else, it would have provoked outright rebellion and, probably, a split."

The 1973 election campaign was fought on a joint platform with Fine Gael. The serious talks had begun a year earlier. Eventually they agreed a 14-point joint programme for Government. Fine Gael won 54 seats and Labour 19 (up one on the 1969 result). Fianna Fáil, which had been through the trauma of the Arms Crisis lost six seats.

When the new Government was announced Brendan Corish was appointed Tánaiste and Minister for Social Welfare. When it came to the appointment of the Labour Ministers, Corish made it clear that he would make the selection himself. Up to then, in the two previous Coalitions, the Ministers were appointed by a vote of the Parliamentary Labour Party (PLP).

Among his appointees to office were two future leaders of the party. Michael O'Leary was given the Labour portfolio, while Frank Cluskey was appointed Parliamentary Secretary to Brendan Corish at Health and Social Welfare.

Corish showed his skills as a leader by not being afraid to recruit and appoint to office people such as Conor Cruise-O'Brien and Justin Keating, both of whom would outshine him intellectually. Ironically, one of those who lost out by this centralisation of power in the hands of the Leader was Dan Spring, father of Dick, who was only a few months short of the minimum period for eligibility for a ministerial pension.

The Government got off to a good start with the Sunningdale conference, which brought about the power-sharing Executive in the North. However, this soon changed. It also had a number of embarrassing incidents, such as when Taoiseach Liam Cosgrave voted against, and helped to defeat, his own Government's Contraception Bill.

Another embarrassment was when the President Cearbhall Ó Dalaigh referred an Emergency Powers Bill to the Supreme Court, and the Minister for Defence, Paddy Donegan, described him as a "thundering disgrace".

Brendan Corish had a tough job on his hands, not least in remaining firm in his decision to appoint Conor Cruise-O'Brien as Northern Affairs spokesman.

During this time, Corish, an accomplished Dáil performer, wrote all his own speeches and often spoke from a sheaf of notes containing up to 50 or 60 points. He was no mean performer either when it came to doing his party piece. He was a gifted actor as well as a good singer.

A challenge to his leadership was mounted by Dr John O'Connell (later Fianna Fáil Minister for Health in 1992) who felt excluded from the intellectual circle which ran the party. The move was defused when Senator Fintan Kennedy of the ITGWU told the meeting that if Corish ceased to be Leader, then his union would have to reconsider its affiliation with the party.

The Cosgrave Coalition lasted four years until the Taoiseach called a general election in June 1977. The Minister for Local Government, Jimmy Tully, had carried out a "Tullymander" of the constituencies which was expected to favour the Coalition.

The Coalition made some new proposals and hoped their firm stance on law and order (Paddy Cooney was Minister for Justice) would see them through. Furthermore, the number of seats in the Dáil had been increased from 144 to 148. But the "Tullymander" backfired.

When the votes were counted, Fine Gael had lost eleven seats and Labour two. Fianna Fáil, on the other hand, had one of its biggest majorities ever – 84 seats – under Jack Lynch.

Brendan Corish resigned the leadership of the Labour Party in July 1977.

3
THAT'S MICHAEL O'LEARY

The battle to succeed Brendan Corish had begun many years before he decided to retire in 1977. He was initially believed to support Michael O'Leary, but in later times favoured Frank Cluskey. The contrast between the two men was stark.

Michael O'Leary is a Cork man. Born in 1936, he was educated at UCC where he became active in politics and student affairs.

John Horgan recalls his first sight of O'Leary:

"One autumn day in the late 1950s, in my first year at UCC, one of my fellow students in the college restaurant pointed to a lantern-jawed figure, with a couple of days' growth of beard, seated at another table, dressed in a white roll-neck pullover and talking vigorously about Marx. 'That's Michael O'Leary,' he said, as if no further explanation was needed. Nor, indeed was it – and O'Leary's evident status as a dangerous revolutionary was enhanced by the rumour that the tea cup from which he drank contained, on occasion, whiskey."

O'Leary was first elected to the Dáil in 1965 for Dublin North-Central and took up a post as liaison officer between the Labour Party and the ITGWU. It was O'Leary who proposed the "no Coalition" motion at the Labour Conference in January 1969, claiming it was a matter of principle for the party. However, he changed his mind when the party failed to make the expected break-through after the 1969 general election.

As Minister for Labour in the 1973-77 Government he had performed well. He was responsible for much of the reforming legislation which was introduced, including new laws on women's rights and industrial legislation. A highlight of his term was when he succeeded in negotiating the National Wage Agreement in 1976.

Frank Cluskey was six years older than Michael O'Leary. Born off Dublin's Dorset Street, he had a number of odd jobs, including polishing milk churns and parading greyhounds at a dog track, before becoming an apprentice butcher at the age of 16.

While working as an apprentice in the city abattoir, Cluskey learned a few facts about mankind. On a cold winter's morning when all the butchers were huddled around the stove it was often difficult to get a space near the heat. Cluskey learned an old trick of seeking permission to have temporary access to the stove to light a cigarette. While there he would quickly drop a loaded stun-gun cartridge inside. The explosion would cause everybody to scatter in all directions while Frank would saunter up to the stove and take the best spot at his ease.

Later he became a Branch Secretary of the Workers' Union of Ireland.

He first ran for the Dáil in a by-election in Dublin South-Central in 1958, but was defeated. He was defeated again at the general election of 1961, but made it to Leinster House in 1965 when the party took a seat at the expense of Clann na Poblachta.

He was a member of Dublin Corporation from 1960 to 1973 and served as Lord Mayor in 1968-69.

His selection as Parliamentary Secretary in Health and Social Welfare in the 1973-77 Coalition proved a wise decision by Brendan Corish, and he was one of the few to emerge with credit.

During his period in office, Corish broke precedent when he brought Cluskey personally into the Cabinet meeting room to argue his case for an increase in social welfare spending. According to reports, he threatened to resign on at least one occasion until the

Cabinet found the required money. He also spearheaded the establishment of the Combat Poverty Programme.

Cluskey was not easily understood by people, and it was difficult to read his mind. "Not even his closest associates could ever be really sure about which cards, or even how many, he held in his hand," wrote John Horgan.

In the battle that followed for the leadership, Michael O'Leary could be said to have had the edge as he was a former full Cabinet Minister. But there was no clear favourite.

John Horgan recalls Michael O'Leary canvassing even while he was still a Minister, and before the change of Government. The lobbying continued "in the Dáil restaurant, on the stairs, or anywhere else we happened to meet".

The actual meeting at which the vote between the two candidates took place was quite controversial. On the first ballot each candidate received eight votes. It was said that the timing was unfair as Seán Treacy was still Ceann Comhairle and therefore unable to attend the meeting. His vote – expected to go to O'Leary – would have given a decisive result.

Normally it would be expected that given such a result the two names would go into a hat and one drawn out. The new leader would be the name that remained inside the hat. However, on this occasion the Parliamentary Labour Party decided otherwise, and to have a second ballot. The idea was suggested by Ruairí Quinn. This time one member – believed to be Liam Kavanagh – changed his mind and Frank Cluskey was elected by nine votes to seven. (Dr Garret FitzGerald was elected leader of Fine Gael on the same morning.)

Author David Fitzpatrick wrote: "The Parliamentary Party was led successively by a former commercial traveller (Tom Johnson), a school teacher (TJ O'Connell), a post office worker (William Norton) and a county council official (Brendan Corish). Not until

1977, when the former abattoir worker, Frank Cluskey, replaced Corish, did the Labour Party acquire a leader with the right to wear a blue collar."

Those who are believed to have voted for O'Leary include Jimmy Tully, Michael Pat Murphy, Pat Kerrigan, Séamus Pattison, Dr John O'Connell and North Kerry deputy, Dan Spring.

Frank Cluskey was supported by Joe Bermingham, Brendan Corish, Barry Desmond, Eileen Desmond, John Horgan, Ruairí Quinn, John Ryan and Liam Kavanagh.

O'Leary was appointed deputy leader but became totally ostracised by Cluskey during the next four years. In fact, the two rarely spoke to each other.

Aware that he had been elected only by the narrowest of margins, Cluskey adopted a cautious approach in his stewardship of the party. The danger of causing division was always uppermost in his mind. Things did run smoothly for a while with the Leader anxious to have the support both of the Parliamentary Party and the Administrative Council.

The media was, in the main, hostile. They saw him as a gruff, old style, unfriendly man who was part of the old school of thinking. They would have preferred O'Leary as he would have had a much more progressive image.

Cluskey excelled as a Dáil performer. For many, the highlight of the day was the Order of Business when Cluskey would question the Taoiseach, or a Minister, and then embarrass them with a withering put-down.

But his procrastination in making decisions, particularly on key social issues such as divorce and contraception, irritated many of the more progressive Labour members of the Oireachtas, notably a young Trinity College senator, Mary Robinson.

During his time as leader in Opposition, Cluskey maintained a very close working relationship with Fine Gael, sharing Private

Members' Time with them each week in turn. Inevitably, when the division bells rang on a Wednesday night, Labour would support Fine Gael's Bill, and vice versa. All the time, of course, Cluskey had the next general election in mind, and the need to get second transfers from the Fine Gael candidates.

Frank Cluskey faced his first electoral test in the European elections in 1979. The party won a major victory in Dublin where both Michael O'Leary and Dr John O'Connell were returned as Labour MEPs. The election results were the high point for Cluskey who, like most others, had not expected them to be so good.

However, disaster was to strike Frank Cluskey in the 1981 general election. The party was in a bad financial state and the preparation for the campaign was a shambles.

Cluskey was also in difficulty in his own constituency of Dublin South-Central. He was resolutely opposed to allowing Dr John O'Connell stand with him for fear the latter would vastly out-poll him, and the suspicion that there might be only one seat there anyway.

Dublin South-Central was a new, hotch-potch constituency, consisting of bits of seven old constituencies from the 1977 general election. Cluskey's electoral record had been poor and the opinion polls conducted beforehand showed him to be in real trouble.

Along with the party's Administrative Council, Cluskey tried to get O'Connell to stand in Dublin West, but O'Connell had plans for his son to stand there.

The issue was very badly handled and eventually led to Dr O'Connell defying the Administrative Council and insisting on standing in South Central. He was expelled from the party. However, he was elected to the Dáil, but party leader Frank Cluskey lost his seat. It was a bitter humiliation, particularly as John O'Connell got almost 9,500 votes as compared to just 4,000 for Frank Cluskey. John O'Connell was subsequently elected Ceann Comhairle in the new Dáil.

With Frank Cluskey defeated there was little opposition to Michael O'Leary taking over the leadership of the Labour Party, although he had lost a lot of friends because of his hostility towards Frank Cluskey. Some would argue it was, in effect, election by default.

Dún Laoghaire TD Barry Desmond, and Michael D Higgins, who had been elected to the Dáil for the first time in Galway West, both indicated that they were interested in throwing their hats into the ring, but there was little support for them.

Eileen Desmond and Liam Kavanagh came out openly in favour of O'Leary and the matter was then only a formality. He became leader of the Labour Party on 1 July 1981.

The new Labour Party Leader was faced with negotiating a Labour Party programme for Government with Fine Gael, a programme to which he had very little commitment.

During Frank Cluskey's leadership he was rarely seen around Leinster House, and hardly ever following his election to the European Parliament in Strasburg.

Negotiations for Coalition took place with Garret FitzGerald at the home of a mutual friend, Gabriel Hogan, a car business man who lived in Sandymount.

Getting the go-ahead for Coalition was not so easy, however. Although Brendan Corish had put the decision in the hands of the party Leader and the Parliamentary Party "in conjunction with the Administrative Council", a "Cluskey compromise" had been inserted at the 1979 conference in Killarney.

This formula compelled the Leader to seek the approval of a special delegate conference for any proposal to join Government. The compromise specified that such a conference should be held between the date of the election and the meeting of the new Dáil.

The conference took place on Sunday, 28 June, the same day that the Fine Gael Parliamentary Party approved the programme.

Over 1,200 delegates attended the conference in the Gaiety Theatre, Dublin. After a long debate – at which Michael D Higgins spoke vehemently against Coalition – the programme was adopted by a vote of 737 in favour, with 487 delegates opposed to it.

Garret FitzGerald was subsequently elected Taoiseach with Labour support by 81 votes to 78. However, it was an unusual Dáil because two seats had gone to H-Block candidates, Kieran Doherty and Paddy Agnew.

Labour got four seats at the Cabinet table (the party had 15 Dáil Deputies as against Fine Gael's 65). Michael O'Leary was appointed Tánaiste and Minister for Energy. He also had responsibility for the industrial side of Industry and Commerce.

Labour's other portfolios went to Liam Kavanagh (Labour), Eileen Desmond (Health and Social Welfare) and Jim Tully (Defence).

As part of the Coalition bargain, Labour also got three Junior Ministries. The Junior Minister for Justice was the new deputy for North Kerry, who was appointed to office on his first day in the Dáil. His name was Dick Spring.

4

THE RAMBLING HOUSE

On the evening of 9 March 1993, a group of neighbours from the parish of Lixnaw in Co Kerry were participating at the Station Mass in the home of local man Sonny Egan.

The custom of the annual "Stations", once a familiar sight in Irish homes, is rapidly dying out, and can only be found these days in rural areas.

"The Mass is ended; go forth in peace," said the parish priest, Fr McElligott, an elderly man who still retains a healthy interest in one of the favourite pursuits of the region, greyhound racing.

When the Mass was over the priest disrobed and sat at a table. In front of him were the names and addresses of the parishioners, and the amount of "dues" owed by each. One member of each family quietly queued up in front of the table as their name was called out aloud, and paid over the amount specified. The money goes to the upkeep of the clergy and the running of the parish. After he had reached the last name, Fr McElligott was invited into the dining-room where a meal had been prepared for him.

Sonny Egan, meanwhile, with typical Kerry hospitality, had a drink for everybody, accompanied by a carefully prepared and presented meal. His house is famous throughout Co Kerry. It is known far and wide as the "Rambling House", where people gather every Tuesday night during the winter months to hear stories and song.

A huge "Céad Míle Fáilte" sign, emblazoned across the fireplace, welcomes guests to the giant-sized hearth, with its turf fire in full blaze.

It is unique in the county. There is no admission fee. Neighbours bring food for everybody. There is no alcohol and the "craic" often continues until four or five in the morning. There is, of course, no hurry home.

So successful is the Rambling House that Sonny Egan has built on an extension to facilitate the crowds. On Tuesday, 9 March, it was packed to capacity.

Sitting quietly in one corner of the house was a local woman, Mrs Dick Laide. Her sister-in-law, Anna Laide, is Dick Spring's mother. The Laides live just a few hundred yards from the Rambling House. Another neighbour is the Fine Gael TD for North Kerry, Jimmy Deenihan.

The house in which Anna Laide grew up, a thatched farmhouse, is no longer standing, and the family now live in nearby bungalows.

It was here, to his uncles, that the young Dick Spring would come during his holidays from school in Tralee. He became familiar with the life of a small farmer, tending cows and cattle. During the summer months he went to the bog and cut turf. Sometimes he would lend a hand to the neighbours.

One of them, Jim Harmon, nowadays a regular at the Rambling House, remembers bringing the young Dick to help him cut turf on nearby Keel Mountain.

The people of Lixnaw are a tough, hardy breed. Nowhere did this toughness show itself more fully than on the hurling field, where winning was sometimes seen as a matter of life or death.

The area is slightly unusual in that it boasts two hurling clubs (Gaelic football is the traditional Kerry sport), Lixnaw and Crotta O'Neills. The Crotta club has a tough reputation. Back in the 1930s two local men, Florrie McCarthy and Jimin Flaherty, dressed up as women and togged out with camáns to help their camogie team to victory against particularly difficult opposition. As well as playing themselves, the women supported the menfolk against all opposition.

"The women were worse than the men playing on the field," says one man from another local club. "They would have flash lamps covered in their scarves and would hit you a lash across the head with them. It was dangerous to get in their way!"

The Laides played hurling and supported Crotta, and this was the club that the young Dick Spring joined while on holidays.

Dick's place generally was centre-field among the 15, and it was in this position with Crotta that Fine Gael Dáil deputy Jimmy Deenihan (the holder of five All-Ireland Football medals) was first given a taste of Dick Spring's "skills".

The match was a tournament against neighbouring Lixnaw. Tension, as usual, was high as the teams lined out against each other on the GAA pitch in Abbeydorney. In order to intimidate the Opposition, Spring pulled on Deenihan with his hurley – before the ball was thrown in. Deenihan will never forget it.

"Dick pulled early," is how the GAA star delicately puts it.

The ploy worked apparently, and Crotta won the tournament.

Dick Spring went on to play hurling with Crotta in a county championship in 1980 against Ardfert (Crotta lost), and he once played with the county hurling team against Wexford.

But it was back in his home town of Tralee that Dick Spring had first learned to play hurling and Gaelic football. His father, Dan, had played for Kerry in 1939 and 1940 before he was married.

Young Richard (he only became known as Dick many years later in Trinity College) was born into a well-run family home on Tralee's Strand Road on 29 August 1950.

As Dan Spring was away for much of the week on Dáil business, it was his mother, Anna, who organised the six children. The family did not take holidays and Dan Spring's summer break was to go out to the bog and save the turf for the following winter.

Most of the family's money was spent on educating the six young

Springs – Arthur, Donal, Dick, Maeve, Kay and Noelle.

The family did their homework at one end of the table in the kitchen which looked out onto a backyard. Their mother looked after constituency work at the other end.

People called to their home all the time. Every problem that humankind can plead to have solved arrived at the door. Dick Spring knew it all before he was very old.

Even during Christmas dinner neighbours would be present, talking to distant loved ones on the telephone, as the Springs were the only people on the street to possess a telephone.

Dick's first school was the Christian Brothers Primary School in Clounalour in the late 1950s. It was there he first made contact with two teachers who were to have a major influence on him, Br Doohan and Michael Hayes.

Michael Hayes had been teaching in Moneenroe National School, in Castlecomer, Co Kilkenny, before transferring to Tralee in January 1961. He was Dick Spring's teacher in fifth class.

He remembers Dick as a very smart, bright young man, with a keen interest in sport.

Michael Hayes took more than an average interest in the welfare of his pupils. He regularly called round to the homes of the boys to consult with their parents.

Today he can still remember Anna Spring sitting around the long table with her children. "She would examine Donal in his Irish, then Dick in his spellings, Maeve in her sums, and so on around the table," he recalls.

One day, when Dick was nine, Anna Spring called to the school to see Michael Hayes as she was not satisfied with Dick's progress. Michael told her that Dick was the boy he put in the chair at the top of the class whenever he had to leave the classroom. "He'll be a leader of men yet," he told Mrs Spring.

In the evenings, Michael Hayes would invite any young boys

who wished to come down to the local green and play football for an hour. Often the young Risteard Mac An Earraig joined in the fun.

Michael Hayes organised games against other schools near and far. The Tralee lads were the dread of many a school. They won every competition and every tournament.

He once organised a game against his old school in Castlecomer. Such was the skill of the Tralee team that in order to "even up" the sides, the Tralee under-12 team played the Castlecomer under-14 side.

Michael Hayes still remembers the team setting out from Tralee, aboard four grey Volkswagon cars, local TD Dan Spring being one of the drivers called in to lend a hand.

"It was like a funeral, looking at the four grey cars," recalls Hayes.

On another occasion, Michael Hayes bought 30 Rail Rambler tickets during the summer for the boys. They visited Dublin 10 times in 14 days!

"I had seen a film myself, *How The West Was Won*, and I thought the boys would like it," he remembers. "We all arrived in due course at the Cinerama on Talbot St, but we couldn't get in as it was full.

"The porter was sorry but arranged for us to go across to the Adelphi to watch *The Nutty Professor*, but he told us the next time we were up in Dublin we could get in free of charge. We were back in Dublin two days later!"

While in Dublin the boys played all sorts of games, from football to basketball. "In the school we always had a spirit of excellence, and we believed that if you were good at sport, then that ability would transfer into that person's position in later life. A number of the great Kerry players are consequently in very good jobs today."

The CBS school put an unrivalled bunch of Gaelic football

stars through its hands. In the period 1960 to 1990 alone, it can claim 35 All-Ireland football medals – Ger Power (8), Mikey Sheehy (8), John O'Keeffe (7), Sean Walsh (7), Ger O'Keeffe (4) and John McElligott (1).

A former classmate of Dick Spring's, Tim Sheehan, today pays tribute to Michael Hayes as an exceptional teacher: "It was he who was really behind all those medals. He transformed the school completely."

Michael Hayes is now retired from teaching, but lives close to Dick Spring's home. He is very proud of his former pupil. He uses three adjectives to describe the Tánaiste: "Honourable, educated and cultured."

Strand Road, the former home of Dick Spring, is in the heartland of the Kerins O'Rahillys GAA club. It was natural for Dick Spring and his two brothers, Arthur and Donal, to join up.

Dick came under the influence of two men there, John Kissane and Christy Griffin, who were to be major influences on his football career.

The club was then one of three (there is now a fourth) in the town of Tralee which has boasted former GAA greats such as Denis O'Sullivan, John Dowling and Sean Walsh.

Today's Kerry selection has two representatives from Kerins O'Rahillys – Noel O'Mahony and Morgan Nix.

However, despite its impressive line-up of players, Kerins O'Rahillys has failed to win the county championship since 1957. It did get to the semi-final in 1974 when Dick Spring played with them.

Dick Spring impressed the county selectors and won a place on the Kerry county team in 1974, the dream of every young Kerry boy growing up.

In 1975 he played in a match against Offaly, and was a sub against both Cork and Dublin the same year. In the match against Offaly he played wing back. Jimmy Deenihan, from the Finuges club, was corner back behind him on the field.

"As a Gaelic footballer he probably lacked the finer skills of the game, but he certainly made up for it with tenacity," says Deenihan. "He was a strong tackler but maybe that was a transfer from rugby. He was at all times very competitive."

However, Dick Spring's decision to go to America meant that his football career ended abruptly in 1975, and he missed out on the great Kerry four-in-a-row team of 1978, 1979, 1980 and 1981.

In an interview with *The Irish Times* in 1982, he attributed Kerry's success in football to its isolation from the rest of the country. "Kerry in Gaelic is somewhat the same as New Zealand in rugby. Because of the distance from other places, a certain emphasis is maintained. I notice that when families from other parts of the country move to Kerry their children may be interested in soccer or rugby or some other game, but within a few months they are actually totally caught up in football. The schools here also play a big part, of course. Gaelic football will never weaken here, no more than soccer will weaken in Manchester."

For his early hurling career, Dick Spring first played with Austin Stack's GAA Club, the only club at the time to play hurling in Tralee.

The club won a county minor championship in 1967 against Causeway in West Kerry. However, the circumstances were somewhat controversial.

With just two minutes to go and the sides level, the Austin Stack's team scored a goal from a 21-yard free. But when the final whistle blew, the referee declared the game a draw.

There were all sorts of appeals and investigations, but the match was never decided officially and never replayed. None of the team received a medal for their win.

Dick Spring was not the only member of the household to

gain honours in sport. His brothers, Arthur and Donal, were equally if not more, successful. Arthur, a GP, won an All-Ireland minor hurling medal with Kerry in 1963. His favourite sport now is golf and he has represented Munster and Ireland on several occasions.

Injury ensured that Dick and Donal Spring would never be capped on the same Irish rugby team, but Donal was capped six times, as against Dick's three.

5

MOUNT ST JOSEPH'S

North Tipperary cannot boast the awesome beauty of Co Kerry, but the scene from the top-most vantage point of the Cistercian College in Roscrea would satisfy most demands.

To the north, the chain of the Slieve Bloom mountains, to the west, the Silvermines, and to the south the familiar landmark of Carrick Hill.

It was this college that Anna Spring chose in the early 1960s to send her boys for their secondary education.

Having left the CBS school in Tralee, Dick Spring spent his final primary year at Listellick National School before arriving at Mount St Joseph's in Roscrea.

It was an unusual choice of school for the Spring family to make. It was fee paying, although Dick Spring arrived on a County Council scholarship.

In an article in *The Irish Times* in December 1992, writer Nuala O'Faolain quoted one Labour Party begrudger, who said: "Dan Spring was one of us, but Dick went away to boarding school."

But the family had known the president of Mount St Joseph, Fr Patrick Moloney, and Dick's mother was a traditional believer in the idea that the only way to get on in life was to get a good education.

An imposing building in domestic Gothic style, Mount St Joseph's College remains a striking tribute to the genius of its architect and founder, Abbot Camillus Beardwood, and its benefactor, Count Arthur Moore, who wanted it to be a memorial to his son, Arthur, who died in 1900.

It was first opened to students in 1905 under its Latin motto: *Insideat Coelis Animo Sed Corpore Terris* (While keeping our feet firmly on the ground, we constantly strive to direct our minds to God).

Sitting in his office in the early days of 1993 the current president, Fr Kevin Daly, a warm-hearted and kindly monk, remarks that the motto is not a bad one for a young man considering a career in politics. And indeed, as a training ground for politicians, Mount St Joseph's has no equal.

Three Ministers, or one-fifth of the 1993 Irish Cabinet – Dick Spring, Brian Cowen and David Andrews – all went through Roscrea.

David Andrews went to the college in 1950, Dick Spring in 1963 and Brian Cowen in 1973. The Taoiseach, Albert Reynolds, also sent both his sons, Philip and Albert Jnr, to Roscrea.

The college is deliberately small, with just 295 boarders. The presence of the 45 largely self-sufficient contemplative monks in the adjacent Abbey is considered to be the stabilising influence that gives Mount St Joseph's its unique identity.

Responsibility is given to the students at an early age under the "house captain" system. Corporal punishment was never used on the students, the monks preferring to "instil self-discipline and self-respect".

Debate and public speaking are actively encouraged.

In 1977, the English teacher, Liam Maher, held a "trial" of the Coalition Government of the time.

Brian Cowen was articulate in prosecuting the then Government, while Pat Crotty, son of FG TD Kieran Crotty, was equally passionate in defending it.

Both called a number of witnesses during a marvellous night full of vim and vitriol. The event is still remembered today by the staff.

The Classics would have been high on the agenda for all

students. Fr Patrick Moloney, himself a Kerryman, who was also college president, taught Virgil, Homer and Cicero to Dick Spring. Spring, in turn, had great respect for Fr Patrick, a tough but fair man, who believed that "education stops at the grave".

"Involvement meant everything to those fellas," says Fr Kevin Daly. "They had good, inquiring minds. They were active boys in every sense, physically and intellectually."

Brian Cowen was a soccer fanatic, David Andrews was good at soccer and played rugby. Dick Spring's first love was rugby, but he also played hurling and threw the javelin.

"I had been to the CBS in Tralee and was naturally steeped in Gaelic games," Dick remembered later. "I tried to organise a Gaelic football team in Roscrea, but it was a school with a rugby tradition and I never fully succeeded.

"In those days I just couldn't see what these guys were getting out of wallowing around in the mud. Then I agreed to try the game and when I got my first pass I automatically put it over the bar."

After five years at Mount St Joseph's, Dick Spring attained eight honours in his Leaving Certificate.

In the spring of 1993 the new Tánaiste called to see his former president, Fr Patrick, now an elderly monk, but still with sharp faculties. As the Tánaiste entered the bedroom he heard Fr Patrick's voice:

"Spring, for five years we tried to fatten you here, but we made no impression."

By the time he left Mount St Joseph's, Dick Spring had decided he wanted to become a barrister. Anxious to be away from the distraction of old Kerry friends, he opted for Trinity College.

Even at this time, at the end of the 1960s, Catholics were actively encouraged by the Hierarchy to stay away from encountering "the dangers of perversion" in that godless place. They were, in fact, ordered "under pain of mortal sin" not to enter

Trinity without specific episcopal permission.

Labour Dáil deputy Dan Spring stuck to the rules and duly obtained the consent of the Bishop of Kerry, Dennis Moynihan, to allow his son attend Trinity to study law.

Far from escaping from his fellow Kerrymen, Dick Spring was once again surrounded by them in Trinity College, in the centre of distant Dublin. Within three months of his arrival he was elected as a member of the Students' Representative Council in which he had little interest and about whose activities he knew almost nothing.

Dick had been spirited onto the Council by the leader of the powerful Kerry "mafia", Joe Revington, later appointed political adviser to him when he was Tánaiste in Coalition with Fine Gael.

Revington is remembered in Trinity with a certain awe as having brought the art of the rural "cute hoor" to student politics, as he tramped his way in his Kerry boots to the Presidency of the Students' Representative Council.

Spring also made new friends at Trinity, among them a young Clontarf lad named John Rogers, later to be appointed Attorney General at the behest of Dick Spring. Rogers, who was also studying law, used to leave his books in Spring's rooms for convenience.

At that time, John Rogers was a supporter of Fine Gael. In his memoirs Dr Garret FitzGerald recalls that Rogers was then a member of the Fine Gael Youth Movement and that, in 1969, he approached him in an attempt to persuade Dr FitzGerald to move against Liam Cosgrave.

Rogers was a quiet, unobtrusive figure in Trinity who regularly attended the political debates of the College's Historical Society and listened to every word, but rarely uttered a syllable himself. The young Kerry law student quickly lost interest in student politics and concentrated his mind on his studies.

One of Dick Spring's lecturers was someone he was to have much more contact with in later life, Mary Robinson.

Spring also continued to develop his keen interest in rugby. During his time at Trinity he played inter-county football and championship hurling for Kerry, and rugby for Trinity and Munster.

Once he had proved himself at Gaelic games, Dick Spring was determined to prove himself at other sports. For years during his youth Spring had refused to play rugby for ideological reasons. He was conscious of the major cultural break and fearful that he might offend his father, who was closely identified with the Republican tradition.

He finally made the change when he arrived at Mount St Joseph's in Roscrea in 1963. His father grudgingly accepted his son playing a "foreign" game, but refused to attend any of the matches until some years later.

While at Trinity, Spring served as honorary secretary of the rugby club and later as captain, leading his team to victory in the Colours match against UCD.

For all this sporting activity he was made a member of the Knights of the Campanile. This is a body, not as secretive as the Knights of Columbanus, which is reserved solely for those in Trinity who have achieved outstanding distinction in sport.

A self-perpetuating body, it is controlled by the "black ball" system of entry. One black ball, registered by any one member, and entry is forbidden. Nobody blackballed Dick Spring.

He played rugby with Cork Constitution, as well as with Munster. In 1974, for example, he played with Munster against the All Blacks at Thomond Park. Later, when he returned to live in Tralee, he trained and played with Tralee RFC. However, it was in 1979, after a lengthy period abroad, that Dick Spring eventually reached the pinnacle of his rugby career.

He was capped for Ireland and made his debut at Lansdowne

Road against France on 20 January of that year. The sides drew with nine points each. Spring gave a competent performance as full-back.

The next match against Wales in Cardiff Arms Parks was a disaster for the Irish team, and a dreadful experience for Dick Spring.

The Irish were doing well and, unusually at Cardiff Arms Park, were in the lead and controlling the game when the ball was kicked towards the Irish line. Full-back Dick Spring misjudged the flight and did not get there in time. Instead, the ball went to Welsh forward Alan Martin who scored a try and the game was turned on its head. Wales won the game by 24 points to 21, the highest number of points ever achieved by an Irish side in the Arms Park.

Usually Spring was a safe pair of hands as he had shown, for example, in a particularly fine display with Munster against Argentina.

Ed Van Esbeck, rugby correspondent for *The Irish Times,* says there were worse mistakes committed by the Irish team that day in Cardiff, but whoever was to blame, Spring only played once more for his country. That game was against England on 17 February in Lansdowne Road and Ireland won by 12 points to 7. But Spring was dropped from the Irish side in the final match against Scotland against whom Ireland drew.

"People always keep on referring to the fact that Dick Spring never played for Ireland after the match against Wales," says Ed Van Esbeck, "but he did play for Ireland again."

The game against Wales is still a sore point with Spring, thirteen years later.

"I had no problem against the French," he later recalled. "Wales was a freak. I didn't catch one ball, and then of course I got no credit for the 20,000 balls I'd caught on the back pitches in Sandymount. I'd lost confidence in terms of the match. I always said I had a concentration span of three seconds, and the ball never came down for five seconds."

Writing in the *Sunday Independent* on 4 February 1979, rugby correspondent Seán Diffley wrote: "Dick Spring will have nightmares about his mishap which allowed Alan Martin the first Welsh try."

Alan Martin himself, the Welsh second row forward, will always remember the game too. It was his only try ever for Wales, although he kicked many goals. The try was later featured in a BBC video of the 101 best tries of all time. Now a teacher in West Glamorgan, Martin says it is "a little unfair" to continually remember Dick Spring for this mistake. "People never tend to remember the balls you caught, just the one you let slip. I remember Dick Spring as a good full-back. These days I only see him in the news bulletins but I still meet his brother Donal who often organises Golden Oldie sides for the World Tournament in Bermuda."

"We always had a very good relationship with the Irish team. There was a great sense of affinity between us," adds Martin, who was capped 35 times for Wales before retiring in 1981. Today his son, Stephen Martin, plays on the under-19 team for Wales.

But the Cardiff game still haunts Dick Spring. While canvassing during the November 1992 general election in Letterkenny, Co Donegal, a local "smart-alec", recalling the notorious incident, asked Spring: "In what game was it that you dropped the ball?" To which an angry Spring snapped: "Why, how many times did you play for Ireland?"

But, according to Ed Van Esbeck, Spring was an "outstanding" player, and scored one of the greatest tries ever seen at Lansdowne Road in a Leinster Senior Cup semi-final.

Spring remembers it, too, as a compensating highlight; the more so since it was witnessed by his American wife, Kristi, who had stood in the rain, understanding little other than the loud abuse her husband was receiving from the opposition supporters.

When Dick scored the try, Kristi happily returned the abuse in kind. Spring went on to captain Lansdowne for the Cup in 1979 before retiring.

"He had an extremely good Cup campaign after the international series, which is some tribute to him," says Van Esbeck, "including scoring a great try against Blackrock in the replay. His career was not a flash in the pan, it spread out over ten years. Most people don't end up with three caps!"

6

A SAWN-OFF SHIRT AND OTHER APPAREL

During the long summer breaks at Mount St Joseph's and Trinity College, Dick Spring travelled to England to work on the building sites to earn some money for his upkeep.

For much of the time he worked for another Kerry "mafia" chief, the builder, John Murphy. Spring did all sorts of work, digging ditches, mending roadways and working on the oil pipeline for the North Sea.

"I worked so much with Murphys on the London building sites, they thought I was one of their own," he joked later. "I did the buildings during the day and bar-tending at night. I wanted the money."

Less educationally endowed co-workers – frequently Irish – were surprised to find one of their numbers reading *The Guardian* newspaper during tea breaks rather than the normal diet of downmarket British tabloids.

When he first went to England, Dick Spring stayed with his mother's sister, Nell Laide, who was married to Moss Lyons. The couple lived on Berker Street, The Villa Cross, in Birmingham and regularly kept young Kerry lads who came over to work on the building sites.

Dick met Frank Quilter from Lixnaw there, a student of agricultural science at UCD. He was to turn up later as a top-class election strategist for Fine Gael in North Kerry, and he was the prime mover behind the spearheading of the successful election of Jimmy Deenihan to the Dáil.

Quilter also stayed with Nell Lyons and drank with Spring and the other Irish workers in the Observatory bar.

The group spent one summer in 1967 laying cable in Stoke-on-Trent. Quilter was the tea-boy, having replaced an unpopular predecessor, dismissed from that particular task because of his lack of hygiene.

The first task of the tea-boy at 7am was to drive around in the dumper and pick up the traffic cones before the day's work began.

"Then," recalls Quilter, "I used to drive like hell in the dumper to the local butcher where I would buy up to 60 steaks for the lads. Before I left I would have a good fire going, so that all would be ready when I got back.

"I would grill the steaks over the fire along with some onions and have the lot ready for the tea break at 10am. This was the first, and for many the only substantial meal of the day. Most of them would go to the pub for lunch. It was rough food, served on greaseproof paper, but it was nourishing."

Dick Spring's job was dumper driver, collecting bits and pieces here and there and delivering them as demanded on the site. One Friday evening the truck had loaded up ready for home when Quilter spotted Spring working away in a completely unhurried fashion in a trench. Quilter was in a hurry as he had a second job as a barman to attend to.

"I got down into the trench to let off water we had been diverting during the day. I called on Dick to get up out of the trench, but he paid no heed. I didn't wait any longer but let in the water. Dick got soaked to the skin in minutes. He turned on me in a rage and attacked me with his fists down in the trench. We didn't speak to each other for days after."

Years later at an election count in Tralee, Spring would jokingly say to Quilter that he bitterly regretted he had not finished him off with a shovel in the trench in Stoke so many years before.

Another character among the Birmingham group was 'Big' Oliver Ryan, from Rathmore in Co Kerry. A loyal follower of Spring's, it was Oliver's custom to buy a new shirt each Friday evening after work and discard the old, dirty one. According to Frank Quilter, if the local girls suspected you worked with Murphy, you had "no chance". The plan was always to disguise yourself and let on you were over on holidays with a relative. Oliver Ryan would then enjoy himself for the weekend before arriving back for work early on Monday morning, with the new shirt intact.

In a regular ritual he would proceed to take it off and spread it out on the roadway. He would then start up the powerful compressor and cut off the sleeves with the jackhammer, and was ready to begin the week's work.

When Dick Spring graduated from Trinity College and the King's Inns with an Arts degree and a BL, he decided to head for New York. Temporarily bored with life in Ireland and Britain he wanted to sample a different way of life.

He worked in bars on the glitzy east side of New York at night for two years. His days were filled with golf or rugby, and occasionally he went skiing.

"It was very good actually, not being in a position to set up my own law practice and making a couple of thousand dollars a week," he recalled later. "I did make enquiries in New York and Colorado about doing Law there but it would have meant going back to college."

He played for New York Rugby Club in the summer of 1976, and already there were signs of a short temper. In an interview with Nuala O'Faolain in *The Irish Times* he recalled playing a rugby match in Rhode Island.

The game became so dirty that he called over the referee and gave him a lecture. The referee, in turn, called for clean play and re-started the game. Two minutes later Spring lost control and got "dug into" an opponent. The referee stopped the game again and asked Spring what he thought he was doing – one minute insisting on high standards, the next minute letting them down himself.

"And that's the end of the story," wrote O'Faolain. "Dick Spring left it at that. He didn't interpret it. It is perhaps not to be interpreted but, like any paradox, simply accepted."

In the summer of 1976 Dick Spring got a job tending tables in the Mad Hatter bar, which is on Second Avenue in the Upper Seventies of Manhattan. One of the patrons of Mad Hatters was a young airline hostess with what is now Trans America Airlines. The woman, Kristi Hutcheson, had just given up a job teaching disadvantaged blacks in Richmond, Virginia. They met in May of 1976 and were introduced by a room mate of Dick's.

"Jerry, another Irishman, introduced us," Kristi recalled. "It was just 'This is our new waiter, Dick Spring.' We really didn't get to know each other that well until later on, around Thanksgiving. I was involved in a court hearing and so I was around New York more, and we became friendly then and throughout Christmas."

The couple quickly fell in love and decided to get married the following February, which they did in Kristi's home state, Virginia, in June 1977.

Their honeymoon gave Kristi her first insight into what lay ahead. "We were married on a Saturday and he left on Monday to come back to Ireland to campaign for his father in the general election of that year.

"I knew right from the start that he was going back to Ireland and that was one reason I never thought about a relationship going any further until we decided to get married.

"I knew that his father was in politics and that he had to go back after our wedding, and that he felt strongly about it. It wasn't until several years after I came to Ireland that I began to really understand what was involved."

Later in 1977 the couple left New York and moved back to Ireland. They rented a house in Blackrock, Co Dublin, and Dick started out as a barrister on the south-western circuit, making regular appearances in Killarney, Listowel, Limerick and Ennis. One fellow-barrister described him as "competent".

Using her own skills, Kristi got a job in Dublin teaching emotionally disturbed children at the Cluain Mhuire family centre, run by St John of God Brothers.

"The first six months were difficult because I missed my family and friends, and it seemed to rain all the time," she said.

Two years later, in 1979, Dan Spring gave up his county council seat. His son, Dick, ran in his place and he was elected to both Kerry County Council and Tralee Urban District Council.

There, it is said, he briefly achieved notoriety when he claimed that the "Hail Mary" should not be said before each meeting of Tralee UDC.

Dick and Kristi Spring moved to Tralee where they bought a modest house on the edge of Cloonorig Estate on the outskirts of the town.

The couple knew that Dick's success in the elections to the local councils was just a prelude of things to come. The big break came in the summer of 1981 when Dan Spring decided to step down in favour of his son.

Fine Gael, desperate to try to regain a seat, ran two candidates, one Tralee-based, to try to win votes away from the young Spring. Spring ended up being one of four Tralee-based candidates – the others were Tom McEllistrim (FF), Denis Foley (FF) and Frank Harty (FG). In the end, Dick Spring held on by the narrow margin of 144 votes over Fine Gael's Ger Lynch, who was Listowel-based.

Dick Spring was a fully-fledged TD, ready for Dáil Éireann and all that it would entail.

7

TÁNAISTE

Dick Spring will never forget Tuesday, 15 December 1981. It was the morning he nearly died.

In office just a few short months and appointed a Junior Minister for Justice on his first day in the Dáil, life had been hectic. On the Monday night previously he had attended two functions. First, he had been to Limerick to present the AnCO Apprentice and Trainee of the Year award. Then it was a mad dash to his home town of Tralee to attend a special meeting of the Urban District Council. But he had the comfort of a State car and Garda driver (they were later removed by Dr Garret FitzGerald in the 1983-87 Coalition and replaced by owner cars and two civilian drivers).

One of Spring's drivers, Garda Edward O'Donovan, was a native of Tralee. His father, Brendan O'Donovan, was a former Garda and lived at St Brendan's Park in the town. They left Tralee in the early hours of Tuesday, 15 December, to head for Dublin. The roads were icy but they made good progress through Limerick and on the Dublin road. At 9am they drove through Nenagh town. There was little traffic and they continued to make time.

One mile outside the town, at Islandbawn, tragedy struck when they collided with another vehicle. The impact was severe and the cars were thrown across the main road, hitting a third car parked on the grass margin.

The passenger in the second car, 51-year-old James Curran from Tonlagee Road, Dublin, was killed. His driver, an off-duty Garda,

Eamon Doherty, from Raheny, was injured. Both men had been on their way to the Limerick greyhound sales. Both Dick Spring and his driver survived the impact. But Spring was seriously injured.

He remembers the moments just before the crash, then regaining consciousness after the impact, discovering the door wrapped around his right arm, his feet buckled underneath him and ferocious pressure on his back.

A team of gardaí were on the scene within minutes, led by Inspector Patrick Moriarty of Nenagh Garda Station.

"On December 15 the lights nearly went out for me," Spring said later.

He was lucky in that an ambulance happened to pass soon after the accident, although the journey to hospital was "horrific". The light seemed to flicker, his blood pressure fell and a sudden coldness fell over him.

Both the Minister and his driver were in the car for 20 minutes before being cut free by Nenagh fire brigade. They were taken to Nenagh General Hospital. An initial examination showed that Dick Spring had sustained a broken bone in his forearm and an injury to a bone in his back.

Later in the day Kristi Spring arrived in Nenagh to visit her husband as did his brother, Dr Arthur Spring.

Writing in the *Irish Independent*, political correspondent Chris Glennon said some of his close friends felt that a week after the accident he would not survive. Later they attributed his recovery to his sheer physical fitness.

The accident was to be a turning point in Dick Spring's life.

First, it ended all involvement in competitive sport, which had been a lifelong interest. The crash also had a profound effect on his wife.

"I do not look at anything in my life as though it is going to last for years and years," she said later. "Our lives have changed so much in the past 18 months and the crash certainly pointed out to us just how fragile it all is. We just get on with living, and we have been living in such an unstable environment."

Dick Spring was compensated in due course. The case, listed for hearing in Limerick Court in April, 1984, as: *Spring v the Minister for Finance and the Attorney General,* was adjourned and subsequently settled.

Answering a question in the Dáil in 1986, the then Minister for Justice, Alan Dukes, revealed that the total cost to the State was £401,765. This figure included a personal settlement with Spring of £170,000. It was a good settlement, but it highlighted the difficulty which arises when a member of the Government is the plaintiff, and the Government is the defendant, with the decision being made by the Attorney General, in this case, Peter Sutherland.

The accident left permanent damage to Dick Spring's back, and to this day he cannot stand for long periods of time. However, regular physiotherapy and swimming have eased the pain considerably. He still manages the odd round of golf.

The crash, which necessitated a rest, interrupted his start in Government. For a while after the accident he feared travelling in cars and instead commuted to and from Tralee by train. But the rattle of the pre-inter city trains caused him great unease and he would arrive in Leinster House in a very pained condition. There, some of the Labour office staff helped to remove the awkward, incongruous-looking steel cage which covered his spine, and lay him on a special couch where he would finally get some relief.

Getting the nerve to travel by car again was more difficult. Here the Garda Special Branch helped out by taking him for fast drives on the Naas dual carriageway and helping him to regain his confidence, which eventually he did.

The new Coalition Government had been dogged by illness.

At one of its first meetings the Government failed to get Paddy Harte elected as Leas-Cheann Comhairle as the Dáil vote tied, due to the absence of the Minister for Health and Social Welfare, Eileen Desmond, who was ill. In a break with tradition, the Ceann Comhairle, Dr John O'Connell, used his casting vote against the Government.

The new Tánaiste and Labour leader, Michael O'Leary, deliberately appointed Dick Spring as Junior Minister in Justice with responsibility for law reform when he saw Jim Mitchell, a non-lawyer, was the senior man in the office. The area of law reform had been neglected in the 1970s, mainly due to the continually pressing security matters arising from the Northern troubles.

"I did not know Dick all that well at the time but I knew he was a qualified barrister and would know the system pretty well," says O'Leary. "But the Government did not last long enough for Dick, or anybody else, to make a real impact."

However, he had made plans.

In an interview in *The Irish Times* in the autumn of 1981, Spring committed himself to introducing recommendations made by the Law Reform Commission. "We want to get rid of the non-status of the illegitimate child and all the deprivation they are subjected to," he said.

He also had plans to review the civil legal aid scheme.

Dublin's late night Leeson St also figured on his agenda and he promised to examine how the late-night drinking clubs there continued to operate. He also said he favoured an early referendum on divorce. But the Government became strained and seemed to crack almost before the 1982 budget was drafted.

"It was a desperate time," says Michael O'Leary. "There was constant fighting within the Labour ranks. The issue of Coalition dominated everything. I was aware, too, that Eileen Desmond and Liam Kavanagh had given up safe seats in Europe for the uncertainty of Cabinet posts."

The Cabinet finally managed to cobble together a budget for 27 January 1982, but it collapsed when Limerick Deputy Jim Kemmy and Seán Dublin Bay Loftus refused to support an 18 per cent VAT levy on all footwear and clothing.

Spring, still confined to a couch and unable to move, was unable to get a pairing for the Budget vote and was brought into the Dáil on a stretcher.

Spring knew he should not travel to Dublin for the vital votes. Feeling unwell and advised of the dangers, he decided, according to friends, to telephone Charles Haughey to seek a "pairing", the system whereby Government deputies are "paired" with members of the Opposition. Haughey was unable to see his way to granting a pair, and Spring made the journey to Dublin. The pain was excruciating.

Spring has never forgiven Charles Haughey for this.

In an interview with the *Irish Press* in 1985, however, Spring indicated that it was no longer a major factor.

"That incident left a deep scar which wasn't expressed for a considerable time by me. The chances are that he (Haughey) may not have known what my personal situation was. Anyway, something like that should not be a factor – I've certainly not allowed it to be in our working relationship in the (New Ireland) Forum, for example."

****

On the day following the Budget, Labour held a crucial meeting of the Administrative Council which was now strongly anti-Coalition, although the Parliamentary Party were in the main behind O'Leary, among them Dick Spring.

"I remember taking off my coat during the AC meeting at around 3am and telling them I was prepared to fight for the night," O'Leary recalls. "We were in Government, trying to fight an election and all the time constantly fighting about Coalition. It was ludicrous."

O'Leary did convince the party to hang in for the election and to support a revised budget which excluded children's footwear from the 18 per cent VAT levy.

The subsequent election campaign turned into a kind of pantomime over whether or not they were fighting as a partner in Coalition.

"Oh, yes we are," was O'Leary's persistent tone.

"Oh, no, we're not," was the equally emphatic response from Michael D Higgins, then chairman of the Parliamentary Party.

The strife within the Labour Party saw its first preference vote drop for the fourth successive general election. It had lost nearly half the level of support it had commanded back in 1969.

In North Kerry, however, the story was very different. There the Labour Party vote surged to a new high of 26 per cent, with Dick Spring topping the poll with 8,552 votes and elected on the first count. Fianna Fáil took the remaining two seats, with Fine Gael's Robert Pierse failing to make an impact.

In the aftermath of the February 1982 election, Labour continued in disarray in Opposition (Fianna Fáil went into Government with the support of Tony Gregory and The Workers' Party).

The Administrative Council of the Labour Party had decided that the party should not join in Coalition. The decision was taken just 13 hours before the new Dáil met and was decided on the casting vote of the chairman, Michael D Higgins. O'Leary had finally lost the battle.

The meeting had also decided to support Dr Garret FitzGerald for Taoiseach.

"It was Michael O'Leary who proposed me for the post, a nice gesture in the circumstances," wrote FitzGerald in his memoirs.

O'Leary was furious with the members of the AC who had been able to call the shots even though, in his opinion, many of them would not get 100 votes at the polls. Senior figures, like Liam Kavanagh, who was an outgoing Minister, were not even on the Administrative Council.

Gradually the idea of leaving the Labour Party altogether and forming a new social democratic party appealed to O'Leary.

"I began to lose faith with Labour," he recalls. "I thought of looking for elements within Labour, Fine Gael and Fianna Fáil, as well as outside, that would have a realistic approach on the economy, be not hung up totally on State investment, and who had a peace-led approach to Northern Ireland."

O'Leary met Garret FitzGerald to discuss the idea and while the former Taoiseach initially appeared interested he did nothing to encourage the idea, despite the obvious disenchantment within the Labour ranks.

Spring was sympathetic to O'Leary's plight, but denies that there were any plans for himself and Liam Kavanagh to leave the party and join Fine Gael if Labour decided to reject Coalition outright.

The political arrow continued to point downward for the party. The by-election in Dublin West in May 1982, caused by the departure of Dick Burke as Ireland's EC Commissioner, saw the party's vote collapse with their anti-Coalition candidate, Brendan O'Sullivan, only managing an embarrassing 703 votes, down from Michael Gannon's 2,617 three months before. The Workers' Party candidate, Tomás Mac Giolla, picked up most of the Labour vote in a new pattern of leakage from the party.

But Labour continued to work in Opposition, proposing a number of Bills, including one on curbing profiteering on re-zoning land. However, Fine Gael failed to support it, and the Bill collapsed.

Meanwhile, tension was growing within Fianna Fáil as attempts were made to unseat Charles Haughey. The political crisis worsened as Tony Gregory and The Workers' Party threatened to withdraw their support for the Government.

But the clock was also ticking fast for Michael O'Leary.

At the end of October, Labour's annual conference was held in Salthill, Co Galway. As expected, the delegates divided hopelessly on the issue of Coalition.

O'Leary was determined to sort out the issue once and for all.

"I was trying continually to make the point that I saw the Coalition not as a survival strategy, but purely as a tactical step."

O'Leary failed to convince the delegates and never spoke another word at the conference. In the end, an amendment from former Leader, Frank Cluskey, (he had regained his seat in the February 1982 election) proposing that the decision be put off until after the general election, was accepted.

O'Leary left Galway bitterly disappointed that he did not have a pre-election pact such as those that had brought Brendan Corish and Liam Cosgrave to power. In effect, he interpreted the vote as one of no confidence in himself.

A few days later, on 28 October, O'Leary resigned as leader of the Labour Party. He also resigned from the party altogether and within a few days he had joined Fine Gael.

"Maybe I did not have the patience to weather the storm," he says looking back now. "But you must have some luck with you as well, that is very important."

Paying tribute to O'Leary in 1986, former Labour Deputy Seán Treacy, later to be re-appointed Ceann Comhairle, said O'Leary had "stood shoulder high as a Minister – he has not been excelled by another Minister in recent times." But he criticised O'Leary for leaving Labour with "indecent haste".

Former Junior Minister Joe Bermingham, who had supported

O'Leary, recalled him as "something of a mixed bag".

"He was a man of many good qualities, and some bad ones, who had few real friends. O'Leary seemed to have a bitterness against him even before he became Leader. I think he was a very brilliant man. He never consulted much and he had a terrible habit of making an appointment to meet you and not turning up."

Bermingham also accused O'Leary of giving up too easily.

Meanwhile, Labour was desperately looking for a new Leader, facing straight into yet another general election, the third in eighteen months.

8
LEADER OF THE PACK

It had been expected that Frank Cluskey would once again make a bid for the Labour Party leadership in November 1982, but he decided not to.

Michael D Higgins made it clear that he would be a candidate, as did Barry Desmond, the latter very much aware now that if a younger person became leader, his chances of ever leading the party would rapidly diminish.

There were some doubts about the wisdom of Dick Spring going forward due to his severe crash injuries. But once he made his intentions clear he had the full support of the Munster deputies, who, although numerous, were not enough to guarantee victory.

The three candidates were duly nominated.

When the Parliamentary Party met to elect a new leader, there was a general discussion on the leadership during which Barry Desmond, who had been proposed by Frank Cluskey, withdrew from the contest.

Michael D Higgins received his own vote and that of his proposer, Mervyn Taylor, and Dick Spring got the remainder.

Spring was proposed by Michael Moynihan of South Kerry and seconded by Liam Kavanagh.

A number of factors favoured Spring, not least that he was from Munster, was young, photogenic and had not attracted any unfavourable publicity.

His wife, Kristi, reacted coolly.

"To me Dick is Dick, the man I married," she told *The Irish Times*. "Being Tánaiste is a possibility rather than a probability at this stage."

Spring was a remarkable choice for leadership. Just 32 years old, he was less than a year and a half in the Dáil. The last man to become Leader of the party at his age, William Norton, survived for 28 years.

Spring was given a baptism of fire as a general election was looming and Charles Haughey was making soundings for support in the face of a no-confidence debate. Although Spring needed some time to gather his forces, he shunned any deal with Fianna Fáil. Later he confirmed that there had been two approaches made to him, both by Bertie Ahern. Haughey denied that there had been any approach whatever.

Two days later, the minority Fianna Fáil Government was defeated by 82 votes to 80 and the country was into another election.

Polling day was set for 24 November and it was a short, sharp campaign.

Earlier that month, the Fianna Fáil Government had published a proposed wording to outlaw abortion in a referendum. Fine Gael promised to put it to the people, if elected.

An opinion poll showed a clear six-point lead for a Fine Gael/Labour Coalition. Fine Gael urged the electorate to transfer their votes to Labour, but Labour remained divided on the issue.

The bickering between old foes, Garret FitzGerald and Charles Haughey, reached new limits during the campaign, culminating in a controversy over a Fine Gael proposal for an All-Ireland police force.

The final blow to Haughey came on the last Sunday before polling when Dick Spring made it clear that he would not do business with Charles Haughey.

"I can say point blank that I won't be negotiating with Mr Haughey as leader of Fianna Fáil," he declared.

All eyes focused on the big TV debate between Haughey and FitzGerald. Before it took place, Dick Spring was given a

20-minute interview by Brian Farrell. FitzGerald was reckoned to have won the debate, having lost the previous two.

When the votes were counted, Fianna Fáil got 75 seats, Fine Gael shot up by seven seats to 70, and Labour, although still in some disarray, far from sliding into oblivion, actually picked up an extra seat, bringing their number to 16. Fine Gael and Labour together had a clear majority of three.

In North Kerry, Dick Spring again headed the poll, with almost 30 per cent of the first preference vote. He pushed up his vote from 8,522 in February to 9,724 in November.

Fine Gael again failed to take a seat, with Tom McEllistrim and Denis Foley securing the other two seats for Fianna Fáil. The result was, however, delayed due to a recount. North Kerry was the one blank spot for FitzGerald where he did not have a deputy.

In a brave attempt to turn the tide, the party had persuaded former All-Ireland football star, Jimmy Deenihan, to be their candidate. In true sporting style he put up a brave fight, losing out by only 144 votes in the fight for the final seat. FitzGerald subsequently appointed him to the Seanad.

The huge victory for Fine Gael nationwide resulted in the election of former Labour party Leader, Michael O'Leary, in Dublin South-West, but sitting Deputy Larry McMahon lost out. It was now up to O'Leary's successor, Dick Spring, to decide the next Government.

The first meeting between Dr FitzGerald and Dick Spring took place in a most unusual venue, the Good Shepherd Convent in Donnybrook. The suggestion had come from John Rogers, Spring's old Trinity friend, and the nuns agreed to surrender their drawing room for the day.

"Prior to these talks the biggest thing Spring had ever negotiated was his mortgage," observed *Sunday Tribune* editor, Vincent Browne.

The two Leaders had known each other since the last Government (Spring was then a Junior Minister), but not very well.

Fine Gael's John Kelly argued that the two parties were poles apart and urged a grand Coalition of Fianna Fáil and Fine Gael. But there were no takers.

Labour demanded a National Development Corporation, major increases in capital taxation, a wealth tax and a property tax. They also wanted a referendum on divorce. Spring also demanded that social welfare payments be indexed to the cost of living, and State-led involvement in job creation. Fine Gael, on the other hand, wanted to get the books balanced within four years.

Most Labour deputies favoured compromise, Mervyn Taylor was the odd man out. He argued that the party should support a minority FitzGerald Government. Spring made it clear where he stood from the start: "I am far more interested in sharing power and having Labour Party policies implemented than in propping up some other party," he declared.

The October Conference in Galway had mandated him to negotiate alone on Labour's behalf.

The two men consulted their advisers of course, FitzGerald mainly with Jim Dooge and Alan Dukes, and Spring with John Rogers, Joe Revington and Pat Magner from Cork (later appointed a Senator). Each morning the Labour team met in Rogers' flat in Ballsbridge for breakfast to decide strategy.

As the talks progressed, much of the work on a proposed pro-perty tax was done by Eithne Fitzgerald (now a Junior Minister) who was an economist and a daughter-in-law of Dr FitzGerald's.

Both FitzGerald and Spring brought along their deputy leaders briefly, Peter Barry and Barry Desmond respectively.

On one occasion Spring brought along Frank Cluskey, the former anti-coalitionist "to frighten the shit out of Fine Gael", as one Labour adviser put it.

Labour won their demand on the indexation of social welfare payments, property and capital taxes, but failed to get divorce through. All that was secured was a promise of an Oireachtas Committee to examine the problem.

On the upcoming referendum on abortion, Spring insisted on the right of a free vote for his party.

In the run-up to the election, Spring had not been backed into a corner on the referendum. He consulted widely about it with his brother Dr Arthur Spring, and barristers John Rogers and Dermot Gleeson, among others. The general feed-back he got was that there were serious defects with the wording.

Before putting the Coalition package to a special conference in Limerick, Spring had to first go through the motions of having talks with Charles Haughey. One of the matters discussed was Haughey's herd of deer on Inisvickillaune, his privately-owned island off the Kerry coast.

A total of around 1,400 delegates turned up for the Labour conference in the Savoy in Limerick on Sunday, 12 December 1982. At the end of the day Spring emerged with his package by a vote of 846 for Coalition, with 522 against.

On the same day Fine Gael's Parliamentary Party accepted the package at a meeting in Dublin.

Then it was down to forming a Cabinet.

There was already agreement that Labour would get the same number of Ministries – four – as in 1981. Spring himself opted for the Environment. Barry Desmond got Health and Social Welfare, Liam Kavanagh took Labour (as he did in 1981), while Frank Cluskey got Trade, Commerce and Tourism.

FitzGerald asked Jim Dooge to serve again as Minister for Foreign Affairs, but he refused. Peter Barry took over instead, and Alan Dukes got Finance, much to John Bruton's annoyance.

The other Fine Gael Ministers appointed were: Michael Noonan (Justice), Gemma Hussey (Education), Austin Deasy (Agriculture), Pat Cooney (Defence), Paddy O'Toole (Gaeltacht, Fisheries and Forestry), Jim Mitchell (Posts and Telegraphs), John Bruton (Industry) and John Boland (Public Service). Peter Sutherland was appointed Attorney General.

Most disappointed of all at not getting a Cabinet seat was Michael O'Leary. FitzGerald and O'Leary had three separate meetings on the issue but the incoming Taoiseach was given a strong message from both parties that O'Leary was not acceptable in Government.

"It is one of the unattractive features of politics," wrote FitzGerald, "that a person who crosses the floor to join another party is rarely *persona grata* thereafter with the party he has left, nor in many cases wholly acceptable, at least at first, to the party he has joined."

When the Dáil met on 14 December, the Coalition's first task was to elect a Ceann Comhairle. Fine Gael's Tom Fitzpatrick was elected on a vote of 86 votes to 80.

It was with some trepidation that Garret FitzGerald faced into Coalition Government with a man younger than his own eldest son, although the two got along well.

John Foley, then a political reporter with the *Irish Indpendent* (later appointed by Dick Spring to the Government Information Services in the spring of 1993) wrote that Spring overcame an initial awe of FitzGerald and began to deal with him in a tough, uncompromising manner when he felt that the party interests were at stake.

The seating arrangements at the Cabinet table were interesting in themselves. Initially Dick Spring sat to the left of the Secretary to the Government, Dermot Nally, who sat to the left of the Taoiseach. Dr FitzGerald reckoned this was not a good arrangement as there was no "eye contact" between himself and the Tánaiste. So the positions were moved. In the new arrangement Dick Spring sat opposite Garret FitzGerald at the other side of the long oval table.

"I was always amused," wrote the former Taoiseach, "by the manner in which Ministers always sat in whatever place they chose by chance at their first Cabinet meeting – sometimes forging surprising *ad hoc* alliances with the neighbours they found themselves beside."

The Taoiseach and Tánaiste set up a very good relationship.

Education Minister Gemma Hussey was the only woman in Cabinet. In her book *At the Cutting Edge,* she remembers Dick Spring as follows:

"He was quiet, almost brooding. He was capable of sharp, witty comments, but these were delivered in informal sessions. All the time we were in Government, I was conscious of two things: the affection and respect the Taoiseach and Tánaiste held for each other, the almost fatherly concern of Garret for Dick, and the terrific burden Dick carried of acute worry about the malcontents on the backbenches who always threatened revolt when the heat of public hostility rose.

"The combination of his back problems, the crisis in public finances and the consequent strains in the Labour Party gave Dick a bad-tempered, often sulky demeanour which irritated many of us in Fine Gael. With hindsight I feel benevolent towards him, but at that time it was difficult."

Gemma Hussey points out that as a result of their good working relationship, FitzGerald and Spring often sorted out many potentially explosive items before they ever came to Cabinet, often in Garret's basement sitting-room in Palmerstown Road.

9
GARRET'S GARÇON

The agenda of the new Government was immediately dominated by the state of the country's finances.

The national deficit facing the Minister for Finance was almost £1 billion. Unemployment had rocketed to 180,000, a horrific figure in the early 1980s. So bad, in fact, was the financial situation that a mini-budget was introduced on 7 January 1983, in advance of the main budget.

Finance Minister, Alan Dukes, signalled his intention to cut the deficit and Jim Mitchell warned that CIE workers might have to take a cut in pay.

Meanwhile, Tánaiste Dick Spring was back in Dublin's Dr Steeven's Hospital for minor surgery. From his hospital bed he issued a statement disowning the sentiments of his colleagues in Cabinet. He challenged Dukes' proposal that the current budget deficit should be £750 million. It was instead projected at £900 million and ended up being £930 million in 1983.

Serious divisions were already evident within the Cabinet.

A welcome distraction for the Government was the news from Justice Minister Michael Noonan that the telephones of two journalists had been improperly tapped by the previous administration.

Back at the Cabinet table, the Ministers were finalising the budget figures.

Gemma Hussey recalls in particular one 12-hour-long (the meetings got longer as time went on) meeting of Cabinet on Friday, 22 January with "tense, difficult, impossible decisions facing us".

"Dick Spring," she noted, "looked as lost as myself."

The talks continued. On Tuesday, 1 February, the meeting went on so long that a driver was sent out for chips and sausages. The Cabinet ate them out of bags and washed them down with gin from the Taoiseach's private office.

Sometimes after a meeting they relaxed in the Chief Whip's office with a drink.

When they went to Barrettstown Castle in July for a think-in, Dick Spring played poker with Gemma Hussey, Peter Barry, Frank Cluskey, Seán Barrett and a few others.

The 1983 Budget was the harshest in decades, with the top rate of income tax pushed up to 65 per cent. But Labour resistance ensured that there were no major cutbacks.

The Party suffered its first casualty when new Co Louth deputy, Michael Bell, resigned the Whip in order to vote against the Social Welfare Bill which cut benefits for workers on short time.

In February the Government published a wording for the Constitution (Amendment) Bill on abortion, using the Fianna Fáil wording. Labour Minister Barry Desmond refused to introduce it.

The wording read: "The State acknowledges the right to life of the unborn and, with due legal regard to the equal right to life of the mother, guarantees in its laws to respect, and, as far as practicable, by laws to defend and vindicate that right."

The three main Protestant Churches came out against the wording, as did a very vigorous anti-amendment campaign.

The Attorney General, Peter Sutherland, advised the Government that the Fianna Fáil wording was ambiguous. The Government re-considered and in March published a new wording. It read: "Nothing in this Constitution shall be invoked to invalidate any law on the grounds that it prohibits abortion."

The Catholic Church and a number of individual TDs rejected this wording.

On 27 April both wordings were voted on in the Dáil when the Fine Gael wording was defeated by 87 votes to 65.

Nine Labour TDs, the two members of The Workers' Party, three Independents as well as the entire Fianna Fáil party voted against the Fine Gael wording.

Dick Spring and four Labour deputies – Barry Desmond, Liam Kavanagh, Michael Moynihan and Séamus Pattison – supported the Fine Gael wording. Nine Fine Gael deputies abstained.

The Fianna Fáil wording was carried by 87 votes to 13. Eight Fine Gael TDs, four Labour deputies and two Independents voted for it. The Labour deputies who supported the FF wording were: Frank McLoughlin, Frank Prendergast, John Ryan, Sean Treacy and Michael Bell (Independent Labour). The bulk of the Fine Gael Party and three Labour deputies abstained.

In the subsequent referendum campaign Labour called for a "No" vote against the wording. Fianna Fáil and Fine Gael "officially" remained aloof, but the Taoiseach made it clear he would be voting "No", while Mr Haughey called for a "Yes" vote.

Dick Spring had urged rejection of the Amendment despite the fact that one of the most outspoken and conservative members of the hierarchy, Dr Kevin McNamara, was his local Bishop.

In his book *The Crozier and the Dáil* John Cooney pointed out that the Labour leader had matched his courage with the perceptive suggestion that the campaign represented a backlash against the slow liberalising of Irish society.

The Amendment was carried by 841,233 against 416,136. However, the turnout was only 53 per cent of the electorate.

Spring's own constituency of North Kerry saw a massive turnout of 76.3 per cent in favour of the Fianna Fáil wording.

The Constitution had its Eighth Amendment, and a wording

that was to have very serious repercussions in the Albert Reynolds' Government in the spring of 1992 involving the "X" case.

Tension between Fine Gael and Labour manifested itself again and again, almost always between Dick Spring and either Alan Dukes or John Bruton. The subject was, invariably, public spending.

"Although for the most part the tension was institutional rather than personal," wrote Dr FitzGerald, " both Dick and John, as distinct from Alan, had short fuses, and this occasionally led to fireworks at the Cabinet table."

Aside from economic matters, the Government also launched the New Ireland Forum.

Invitations were sent to Official Unionists, the DUP and the Alliance Party as well as other interested groups to come and give their views on the North, but the Unionists and Alliance Parties refused.

The first meeting of the Forum took place in Dublin Castle on 30 May 1983, under the chairmanship of Dr Colm O hEocha, the President of UCG.

There were 27 full, and 14 substitute members.

Fianna Fáil had nine members and four substitutes, Fine Gael eight and three substitutes, Labour five and two alternates and the SDLP five members and five alternates.

The Labour team was led by the Tánaiste, Dick Spring, and included full members: Frank Cluskey, Frank Prendergast, Senator Stephen McGonagle and Mervyn Taylor. The alternates were Eileen Desmond and Senator Mary Robinson.

The Forum received over 200 written submissions and heard oral evidence from 20 people.

The sessions were not without their dramatic moments, however. During a private session on 16 December, Dick Spring accused the Fianna Fáil delegation of being the source of leaks from the Forum to the press. Haughey was infuriated and threatened to withdraw his delegation until Spring withdrew his allegations. Spring refused.

An emotionally distraught Haughey pleaded that no one had suffered more at the hands of journalists than he had, and immediately broke down in tears. He was helped from the room by Fianna Fáil colleague, later EC Commissioner, Ray MacSharry.

During a tense lunch, Haughey and Spring made up, Haughey explaining how hurt he and his family had been the previous day following the publication of a new book, *The Boss*, by Joe Joyce and Peter Murtagh.

"I have just been reading *The Boss*, all about CJ Haughey," wrote Gemma Hussey in her diary of 9 December. "It is the most positively chilling thing I have read in a long time....God bless us, at least Garret is very decent and straight."

The Forum Report was launched on 2 May 1984, and eventually provided the basis for the setting up of the Anglo-Irish Conference.

It proposed three options: a unitary State, a federation, or joint authority.

However, there was considerable controversy over Charles Haughey's interpretation of the findings when he suggested that a unitary state was the only solution realistically on offer.

The Forum Report led directly to the Chequers Summit with Margaret Thatcher where she rubbished all three options with her now infamous remark: "Out..., Out..., Out...."

Back at the Cabinet table, the Government announced that it was removing State cars from the 15 Junior Ministers. Instead they would receive a mileage allowance and two paid civilian drivers. All State cars were to be reduced in size.

In September, Spring threatened to pull out of Government

in yet another row over spending cuts. Eventually, following a crisis meeting between the Taoiseach and the Tánaiste, Spring and his colleagues returned to the Cabinet table, but it had been close. However, Labour's opposition to spending cuts and Fine Gael's opposition to capital taxation meant that the Government stagnated and there was little progress.

Then came the Dublin Gas crisis.

John Bruton, as Minister for Energy, worked out a financial package to save the almost bankrupt Dublin Gas Company and allow it to distribute the natural gas off Kinsale. The package amounted to £126 million.

But Frank Cluskey was staunchly opposed. No way would he agree to the State bailing out a private company. He wanted Dublin Gas nationalised.

A succession of Cabinet meetings failed to resolve the *impasse* and on Thursday, 9 December 1983, Frank Cluskey resigned from the Government. The resignation sparked off a mini-crisis, but Spring acted swiftly. He demanded a re-shuffle of Cabinet portfolios, and demanded Energy for himself.

Bruton was furious and resisted. He even threatened resignation, but Spring emerged the victor, as Minister for Energy. Labour had changed personnel, but had won charge of the increasingly important Energy portfolio.

Liam Kavanagh became Minister for the Environment and Ruairí Quinn, who had been a Junior Minister, came into the Cabinet as Minister for Labour.

John Bruton remained as Minister for Industry, but also took over Frank Cluskey's old portfolio of Trade, Commerce and Tourism.

"We have to keep our heads down, keep calm, keep working and let the Labour Party fall asunder in its own way," Gemma Hussey wrote in her diary of 9 December.

Labour kept up the pressure by opposing harsh cost-cutting measures in the 1984 Budget.

The Budget, when Alan Dukes delivered it on 25 January, was neutral with a few minor adjustments here and there. Again Labour had withstood a Fine Gael effort to reduce food subsidies.

"We divided nothing equally," Dick Spring said of the period later.

In June 1984 came the European elections. They proved a disaster for the Labour Party which failed to win any seats. (The party had held four out-going seats, two in Dublin and one each in Leinster and Munster). The trend was worrying and followed a similar one set by the Dublin Central by-election at the end of 1983 caused by the death of George Colley.

The anti-coalitionists were on full alert yet again.

In his book, *Hiding Behind a Face,* author Stephen O'Byrnes attributes Labour's failure in the European elections to a "woefully amateur organisation".

One of the outgoing MEPs, Brendan Halligan, dropped out before the contest, and then went on to predict that the party would not win any seats. Dick Spring reacted angrily by publicly calling him a "bollocks"!

In an article in the *Irish Independent* on 17 February, political correspondent Chris Glennon wrote that the "majority of Dublin constituencies are virtually bereft of effective Labour party organisation".

Labour were continually under pressure in Dublin from The Workers' Party as well as their own anti-coalitionists.

"The 'Left' are good at shouting, protesting and complaining, but if they went out and did a bit of work building the organisation, they would be helping the party," one of Spring's advisers was quoted as saying at the time.

The lax state of the party was shown in an unexpected proposal from the new General Secretary, Colm O'Briain, that branches without their registration fees paid up to headquarters should be scrapped. A number of deputies were taken aback at the idea, and the result was an extension of the deadline for payment.

O'Briain had been an outstanding producer in RTE, as well as an administrator with the Arts Council, and had shone above every other applicant as Seamus Scally's replacement.

One of O'Briain's first tasks was to sort out the financial problems, mainly caused by the three general elections in a row. The unions' affiliation, about which much noise was often made, was at the time only worth £13,000 per annum, a pittance by any standard.

There was also the growing problem of the so-called Militant Tendency, which began to emerge as an organisation within an organisation. This was to come to a head a few years later.

"Dick Spring needs to look in several different directions at once," wrote Chris Glennon. "Firstly he must watch key FG figures seeking party advantage towards the day when they might be the biggest, single party. He must look at sections of the Labour Party which appear to have in-built self-destruction mechanisms. He needs to look at the machinations of the trade union leaders, whose unions are affiliated to Labour, but whose actions and words indicate a lot less than support, and he must look at his own constituency (the least of his problems)."

To help him do all these things, Spring had around him a small coterie of advisers – Willy Scally, an economist, who had worked for the Sugar Company (now Greencore), Fergus Finlay, a former trade union official, Joe Revington, his friend from Trinity who joked about being a Kerry Protestant married to a Derry Catholic, and John Rogers, the barrister friend, also from TCD days.

Scally was a brother of the former General Secretary of the Labour

Party, Séamus Scally. He was credited with the financial analysis that scuppered Alan Dukes' plans to tinker with children's allowances.

Finlay, who had been living in Cork, was the Assistant Government Press Secretary on the Labour side. He maintained a watching brief for Spring in the media and advised on what was likely to emerge there.

Revington, the former controversial TCD student, was looking after the Kerry constituency where, every second Saturday, clinics began at the Spring home at 10am sharp and continued throughout the day in a network of pubs, hotels and community centres.

Finally, Rogers, although outside the mainstream of political activity, provided a balanced view on what was going on inside Government Buildings.

In this group Spring had a very dynamic and clever political team.

10

HYSTERIA

On Thursday, 2 August 1984 the Coalition Government dropped an unexpected bombshell. It announced a decision to halve the existing food subsidies on butter, bread and milk.

The news broke over the Bank Holiday weekend when all the Senior Ministers were away. Worse still, Frank Prendergast, the Government Press Secretary, was in London for a routine meeting and the Assistant Secretary, Fergus Finlay, was moving house from Cork to Meath and had taken a week's holidays.

"Appalling flak going on about the food subsidies," wrote Gemma Hussey in her diary of 4 August. "The hysteria from Michael D Higgins, Joe Higgins of the Labour Left, John Carroll, the housewives ... the whole thing is pointed straight at the Labour Party. Dick Spring went on radio. He was extremely strong in support of the Government."

Spring was left to handle the crisis almost on his own.

He had underestimated the reaction, fuelled, of course, by Fianna Fáil. But he managed to contact John Boland. Both did an exhaustive round of interviews.

Ironically, the move, aimed at saving some £20 million, was not needed afterwards as the national deficit was less than anticipated.

In the short term, the consequences were disastrous. Overnight Spring's satisfaction rating dropped from 40 per cent to 25 per cent, but he had demonstrated that he was prepared to make, and to take, tough decisions.

Ella Shanahan, a journalist with *The Irish Times*, went to Spring's constituency to sample the reaction.

One woman, who lived in the housing estate close to the Spring home was very angry.

"It's OK for them on the wages they have," she said. "Their food is subsidised by the Dáil. I think Dick Spring should really be in Fine Gael rather than Labour."

Tralee UDC Labour Councillor, Michael O'Regan, was also unhappy.

"I think this is going to have a detrimental effect on him (Spring)," he said. "In my humble opinion, you should never remove something unless you replace it to cushion the under-privileged and the poor. They tell them to tighten their belts. If they tighten them any more, they will be ruptured."

In the eyes of many back-bench deputies, Dick Spring was again the full-back who had dropped the ball in front of his own goal posts. The 20,000 balls he had fielded were forgotten.

But the damage had been done. The Government responded with a three-year National Plan. The launch was a success and a superb piece of public relations work by the handlers. Fergus Finlay suggested the title: "Building on Reality". The document set out the economic parameters for the Government up to 1987.

Launching it, the Taoiseach committed himself and his Ministers to "a new beginning".

"As far as I'm concerned our future begins now," he declared.

In 1985 the Government got round to some more social reform when it introduced a new Bill on the thorny issue of contraception.

In 1979 Charles Haughey had produced what was described as "an Irish solution to an Irish problem", by legalising the sale of contraceptives on prescription for family planning purposes only.

This law had later been found wanting by the European Court in the case of a married woman whose health would have been put in jeopardy in the event of a further pregnancy.

The new Family Planning (Amendment) Bill, a personal triumph for Barry Desmond, allowed for the sale of contraceptives openly by pharmacies and Health Boards to people over the age of 18.

The measure had been delayed in Cabinet because Barry Desmond had wanted the age limit reduced to 16, the legal age for marriage.

The Bill went through but was opposed by three Fine Gael deputies and two in Labour, Seán Treacy and Frank Prendergast. Treacy voted against the Bill, while Prendergast abstained. (On the Fianna Fáil side of the House Des O'Malley abstained and was expelled from the party.)

Dick Spring was visibly angry over the decision of two of his deputies to defy the Bill. The party, he warned, could no longer be used as "a flag of convenience".

General Secretary Colm O'Briain, spelled out the implications:

"The future of the party, as a whole and as a political entity, depends on its ability to act in concert. And clearly, on a matter of Labour policy for over a decade, introduced in Parliament by a Labour Minister, to have two parliamentarians exempting themselves from support of that measure is a considerable body blow to the organisation. But it illustrates a maxim that a smaller Labour Party might be a more effective and cohesive unit than a large unstructured and disorganised one."

Seán Treacy left the Labour Party, reducing their number of deputies to 15. The party claimed he voted himself out of Labour by his action. Treacy claimed he was expelled. He was very bitter about the event.

"I was brought before the leadership – Spring, Desmond, Mervyn Taylor and Joe Bermingham," he said later. "Dire threats were made to me, and even worse to Frank Prendergast. But I gave not a tinker's curse for those people. I was there before them and I will be there after them."

But throughout its tenure, the Coalition was deeply divided over the Social Welfare cuts, the on-going question of local radio and the proposed National Development Corporation.

The local radio issue was particularly divisive as Frank Cluskey (now on the back-benches) insisted that the State should have a 51 per cent hold in every licence granted. In the end nothing was done and the myriad of pirate radio stations continued to flourish.

Relations between Garret FitzGerald and Dick Spring also came under strain in the early autumn of 1984 when the Government had to appoint a new EC Commissioner.

The Labour Party proposed Justin Keating. Fine Gael, on the suggestion of Joan FitzGerald, came up with Peter Sutherland.

Spring eventually agreed, but on condition that he could nominate the new Attorney General.

Dr FitzGerald resisted as, in his view, the AG was always chosen by the Taoiseach of the day. But eventually he gave in.

"I need not have worried," he wrote later in his memoirs. "John Rogers turned out to be excellent, and enormously helpful to me on political as well as legal matters."

Gemma Hussey described him as "young John Rogers, a saturnine, tall fellow".

At the Fine Gael Parliamentary Party meeting on 14 December Oliver J Flanagan launched a bitter attack on Rogers' appointment.

"We all hold our noses when we think of the Labour Party," he declared. Gemma Hussey jumped up and demanded a retraction. Oliver J changed his comment to: "I hold my nose when...."

The Coalition dragged on through 1985 with the proposed National Development Corporation causing a constant rift between Dick Spring and John Bruton.

On Thursday, 18 April, Gemma Hussey reports Dick Spring

behaving "as strangely as I've ever seen him".

The Labour Party had rejected the idea of the NDC as agreed by the Cabinet a week before.

"There have been behind-the-scenes problems resulting in Dick staying up all night alone, thereby getting himself into an exhausted condition," she wrote in her diary. John Bruton was "upset". A few days later, she says of Spring: "Maybe he's too young."

At the Labour Party conference in Cork in May, Dick Spring and his Ministers were given a severe bruising by the delegates. There the real enemy was again "coalitionism".

By the narrowest of margins, Spring avoided having to return to a special conference six months later with a re-negotiated national economic plan. The call was rejected only when crucial help came from Transport Union leader, John Carroll. The fact that fewer than 500 delegates out of a total present of 1,100 bothered to vote at all on a crucial issue showed up a serious failure by Dick Spring to marshal his troops.

At the conference, Environment Minister Liam Kavanagh also suffered the humiliation of having his water charges issue openly condemned by vote.

But Cabinet meetings for the reminder of 1985 tended to be dominated more and more by the upcoming Anglo-Irish Agreement which was signed in Hillsborough on Friday, 15 November.

Four days later, Senator Mary Robinson announced her resignation from the Labour Party because she said the Agreement could not achieve its objective of securing peace and stability within Northern Ireland, or on the island as a whole.

She rejected the Agreement because it would not be supported by any of the Unionist Parties. But she emphasised that she did not want to be "seen in the same bed as Fianna Fáil", because she did not share any of the criticisms which Mr Haughey had advanced.

In a letter to her, Dick Spring said he recognised there were risks in the Government's approach, but there were also risks in doing nothing. He thanked her for the "significant contribution" she had made to the party and "the major role you played in the preparation of the Report of the New Ireland Forum".

A party spokesman described Mrs Robinson's decision as "a bit unusual" as she had not given any indication that it was a resigning issue.

"You have to admire Dick Spring," said one cynical Labour supporter at the end of 1985. "We have lost all our Euro seats and 30 local authority seats. There's no progress on tax and the polls show us at our lowest ratings ever."

But at the end of three years as leader of the Labour Party, Spring was confident and determined to remain as leader "say for another 15 years".

Already he was planning for extra seats in places such as South Dublin, Galway and Wexford. Labour, he promised, would fight the next election independently of Fine Gael.

Facing into yet another budget, he said the "determination" was there to see them through.

Alan Dukes delivered his 1986 Budget Speech at the end of January. It was by far the most creative of the four, and afforded some relief to the PAYE sector.

However, there was uproar in the Dáil the following day when Health Minister Barry Desmond announced that the Government would be closing two major psychiatric hospitals, in Castlerea and Carlow.

Another bombshell struck on 4 February when Mary O'Rourke told the Dáil that Gemma Hussey was planning to close Carysfort College.

"The education world, led by Fianna Fáil, has now gone into a paroxysm of hysterical indignation," Gemma wrote in her diary that night.

The Government gave Carysfort a two-year reprieve, but the damage was done.

Against this background, Garret FitzGerald decided to re-shuffle his Cabinet. He had been planning to do it since the previous autumn but put it back for a number of reasons, not least because a number of Ministers only qualified for pension on 14 December 1985, the third anniversary of the Dáil.

Dr FitzGerald decided that both Gemma Hussey and Barry Desmond would have to move. He also decided to move Bruton back into Finance and link it with Public Service. Barry Desmond would go to Justice and Michael Noonan from there to Industry and Commerce to replace Bruton. John Boland would go to Health and Social Welfare, while Alan Dukes would take Education.

Finally, in an innovative move, Gemma Hussey would be in charge of a new Department of European Affairs, with Peter Barry still Minister for Foreign Affairs, but concentrating on Anglo-Irish matters.

Dick Spring agreed with the strategy of moving one of his Ministers, Barry Desmond. When Desmond was told by the Taoiseach, he refused to accept the change. While other Ministers were told and accepted the Taoiseach's decision, Desmond refused to budge.

In a late-night meeting FitzGerald offered Desmond a range of other portfolios, including Social Welfare on its own. He refused everything, making it clear to the Taoiseach he would have to be fired.

Finally, Spring backed his deputy leader and told the Taoiseach he would resign with his colleagues from Government.

A stunned Garret FitzGerald sat down to prepare a Fine Gael Cabinet. But within half an hour Dick Spring was back with the news that Barry Desmond was prepared to keep Health on its own.

The Taoiseach gave in. He switched Gemma Hussey to Social Welfare. She broke down in tears at the move which she saw as a major demotion from European Affairs. In the final shake-up, Bruton got Finance, but Public Service went to Ruairí Quinn.

John Boland got Environment, and Liam Kavanagh went to Fisheries, Forestry and Tourism. Paddy O'Toole got Defence while retaining the Gaeltacht.

Finally, Dukes got Justice and Paddy Cooney Education.

There was near disbelief in the Fine Gael back-benches as well as in Fianna Fáil.

"Garret has made the most appalling mess of the re-shuffle and I am the victim to expediency and am now Minister for Social Welfare," Gemma Hussey wrote in her diary. For a time she considered resignation, but was advised against it.

It was a bruising defeat for Garret FitzGerald who had failed to get the re-shuffle he wanted. He had also failed to drop anybody or to bring in new blood to the Cabinet.

He did, however, drop three Junior Ministers, Michael D'Arcy, Donal Creed and Joe Bermingham (Lab) in favour of Avril Doyle, Enda Kenny and Toddy O'Sullivan (Lab). The one Labour change was at the initiation of Dick Spring.

FitzGerald had bungled the entire re-shuffle and compounded the problem by misleading the Dáil and the media on what exactly had happened. It was an all-time low for FitzGerald. Dick Spring, however, managed to let most of the flak go over his, and Labour's, head.

****

Divorce was always a thorny issue for the Coalition.

Back in 1981 Michael O'Leary had tried hard to get a referendum on the issue agreed as part of the Programme for

Government, but failed.

The 30-page agreed Programme for Government in November 1982 devoted only three paragraphs to what was called "social reforms". The third paragraph promised: "The reform of the marriage laws will be examined by a Committee of the Oireachtas before the end of 1993, which will recommend on the problems of the protection of marriage and on any legislative or constitutional action that may be required." The time scale was not adhered to, however, but the committee did report in April 1985 and made a recommendation to remove the constitutional ban on divorce.

In November 1985 Michael O'Leary managed to force a Private Members' Bill to a vote, much to the embarrassment of the Labour Members. However, the Bill failed to secure a Second Reading.

Garret FitzGerald favoured divorce legislation, but knew his party was deeply split on the issue.

On Wednesday, 26 February, a Labour Bill was brought before the Dáil but FitzGerald voted against it on the grounds that there should be consultation with outside interests first. In the end only eleven Fine Gael deputies voted with Labour, and the Bill fell. No Minister or Junior Minister supported it, out of loyalty to the Taoiseach.

Shortly afterwards FitzGerald asked Attorney General John Rogers to draw up proposals for a referendum on divorce. The opinion polls showed a huge majority in favour.

The published proposals allowed courts to grant divorce and the right to remarry where there had been a breakdown in the marriage for five years and where there was no prospect of a reconciliation.

The Catholic Church denounced the idea, while Fianna Fáil remained officially "neutral".

The first problem came when Education Minister Paddy Cooney signalled his opposition. The Taoiseach moved quickly by allowing deputies to object in a personal capacity. Cooney was soon joined by the two Junior Ministers in Agriculture, Paul Connaughton and Paddy Hegarty.

Particular criticism was levelled at the failure by the Government to put in place a number of pro-family, pro-marriage measures in advance of the referendum.

Throughout the campaign, Tánaiste Dick Spring argued strongly in favour of a "Yes" vote.

Speaking in Cork on the day before the referendum he clashed strongly with Mgr James Horan of Knock who had accused the Government of proposing to abolish a special clause in the Constitution which guarded the special institution of marriage.

"Untruths like that have to be taken on, head on," declared Mr Spring. He likened some of the language being used by the Church to that used by the Bishops against Dr Noel Browne's Mother and Child Scheme.

But he predicted the result would be close.

"I think you are talking about a margin of 5 per cent either way," he added.

The referendum, which was held on 26 June, was rejected by 935,843 votes against, to 538,279 in favour. The actual turn-out on the day was 60.84 per cent. Only five constituencies – all in Dublin – voted in favour of divorce.

Kerry North, Dick Spring's home base, was one of the areas to vote most heavily against, 19,497 as opposed to 7,210 in favour.

It was a bitter blow for the Government, but most of all for Garret FitzGerald, who had committed himself to introducing social legislation.

The autumn of 1986 saw the Government move into its last period in office. As rows over the budget figures for 1987 began to dominate every meeting, the mood of the Members was exemplified by John Boland who described Richard Bruton's appointment as a Junior Minister in September as "the third mate on the Titanic".

In mid-October Dick Spring was involved in another car accident near Askeaton, Co Limerick.

On the night of 18 October, he was travelling in his State car from Tralee to Limerick dog track when the accident happened at Morgan's South, two miles outside Askeaton.

Mr Spring, his Garda driver, Donal O'Sullivan, and the Tánaiste's two nephews, Richard Laide and Arthur John Spring, all escaped unhurt. All were able to continue their journey in another car.

At the races, Spring's dog, aptly named "Spring One", qualified for the final of the St Leger Stakes when it came second in its heat.

The accident was also raised in the Dáil on 20 November when the Minister for Justice, Alan Dukes, confirmed that a claim had been submitted to the State by the owner of a damaged wall.

Fianna Fáil's Dr Michael Woods said it had been alleged that greyhounds were in the car, and he wondered if they had been injured.

"We have received no claims from any greyhounds," replied Mr Dukes.

The Government crisis worsened as the autumn progressed.

"The political situation is spiralling downwards and can't be controlled," wrote Gemma Hussey in her diary in early October.

The Fine Gael Ministers planned first to part amicably with Labour over the Estimates on 22 October, and then go the country on a tough budget.

Threats by Labour Party dissidents not to support the Government saw climb downs on a number of issues including a directive on equality legislation.

When the Dáil adjourned for the Christmas recess there was still no agreement on the budget figures between both sides, with John Bruton and Dick Spring stubbornly dug in on either side.

The Cabinet had succeeded in reducing spending demands by £350 million but failed to agree on further health cuts in order to get down the deficit figure. Both sides finally agreed to part ways on 20 January 1987. Garret FitzGerald described the occasion as "a sad moment".

A formal vote was taken by the Cabinet at 12 noon after which Dick Spring formally handed the Taoiseach his resignation. All the Ministers shook hands, many with strong emotions. Gemma Hussey, the lone woman on the Cabinet throughout the four years, was warmly embraced by Ruairí Quinn and Barry Desmond.

Outside Government Buildings, Dick Spring told the waiting press that he and his colleagues had resigned. However, the Attorney General, John Rogers, remained in office for the duration of the Fine Gael Government.

Dick Spring, leader of a disgruntled Labour Party, was now facing his second general election.

Some years later Fianna Fáil Government Press Secretary, PJ Mara, pinpointed the split as a major mistake for both Fine Gael and Labour.

"The FG/Labour Coalition was well established with a comfortable, working majority in the Dáil and was respected and popular with the public," he said. "Then the Labour Party blew what could have been the natural order of things for years to come – a FG/Labour Coalition. Now a major question mark hangs over Fine Gael. I don't believe that party has a leadership problem. I believe they have a relevance problem."

11
PRESERVING BEWLEY'S

Remaining in the Coalition Government for four years was an achievement in itself for Dick Spring.

As leader of a party which was continually divided over the Coalition issue, it is a clear indication of Spring's leadership ability to have been able to hold the party together.

And while there was much that was not achieved, notably in the area of public borrowing, there were a number of impressive prizes, particularly the Hillsborough Agreement, the major development in Anglo-Irish relations at that time since 1922. There was also the establishment of the National Development Corporation, limited reform of local government and a new Bord Pleanála outside of political influence.

The party had made a major impact in the area of social reform, but did not receive the credit.

Party General Secretary Colm O'Briain, who took over from Séamus Scally in 1982, saw Labour's dilemma in that it was a middle-sized party:

"Labour's dilemma is that it is a middle-sized party, trying to advance socialist ideological policies in the non-ideological environment of an essentially conservative society," he said in an interview in 1985. "It's a minority party, neither small enough to be called a small party, nor large enough to be a major factor in Irish politics, which finds itself politically caught up in the squeeze of what the Irish people want out of a political system."

But an anti-coalitionist, Joe Higgins, saw matters much more simply. "If Labour was standing as a socialist party... and were to offer and explain clear, socialist policies on how the problems of Irish society would be resolved, then I think Labour would receive overwhelming support and we could rapidly be on the way towards an overall majority," he said, also in 1985.

Certainly if Irish people voted on issues alone, the Labour Party would have commanded up to 40 per cent of electoral support. Much of their problem was organisational and in not having an effective political machine.

Because of its stance, the Labour Party attracted little by way of contributions from the corporate sector, and without money it is always difficult to organise. Its membership subscription was only £1 at the time, and it received a relatively small amount from trade union affiliation fees.

When O'Briain took over as General Secretary, he immersed himself in a re-organisational drive that few had expected, and which was not always welcome.

Once, in desperation, he referred to un-named "personal fiefdoms" within the party, where O'Briain was meeting considerable resistance to his reform plans.

O'Briain wanted to get away from the *ad hoc* election campaign to proper election organisation. He spoke of a 15-year plan.

"One doesn't want to have ridiculous ambitions and unrealistic targets," he said.

But O'Briain resigned in June 1985 as a result of growing mistrust between himself and Dick Spring. (In 1993 he was appointed as a special adviser by the new Minister for Arts, Culture and the Gaeltacht, Michael D Higgins).

He had tried to turn the party round and succeeded in winning back some of the liberal vote which had been going to Garret FitzGerald in the early 1980s. His resignation was a bad blow for Labour.

The appointment of O'Briain's successor was a matter of some controversy.

The advertisement, in September 1985, specified that "this very important post carries with it a rare opportunity to be part of the Labour Party's participation in the Government of this country, and to contribute to it in a very special way."

The implication was that no anti-coalitionist need apply.

However, one did, in the shape of Bernard Browne, an official of the FWUI. The other two contenders were Fergus Finlay and Ray Kavanagh.

Browne was the eventual choice of the interview panel – which consisted of Dick Spring, Bill Attley of the FWUI, John Carroll of the ITGWU, party chairman Senator Michael D Higgins and independent personnel officer Anne Lennon – and his ratification by the party's Administrative Council was expected to be a mere formality. (It is believed Dick Spring favoured Fergus Finlay at the interview stage, but he reluctantly agreed to Browne in order to make the decision unanimous.)

However, Browne gave an unexpected interview in the *Sunday Tribune,* in which he declared himself opposed to Coalition. At the same time, his name appeared on a trade union circular which criticised parts of the Anglo-Irish Agreement, then recently signed by the Coalition Government. The secretary of Browne's union was prominent Sinn Féin member, Phil Flynn.

The AC divided sharply on the matter and referred it back to the interview board and to the party officers.

Spring and his supporters would not accept Browne after his "gaffe", and neither would a minority of the AC accept Finlay as he was seen to be too close to Spring. The compromise winner was a former schoolteacher from Co Offaly, Ray Kavanagh, who was appointed in January 1986.

The appointment marked a new strain between Spring and some

members of the AC. It was seen as a move by Spring to take firmer personal control of the party and to have his supporters in key positions.

Three members of the AC, Sam Nolan, Frank Buckley and Mick O'Reilly, wrote to Spring accusing him of opting for Fine Gael rather than the Labour Party.

"The refusal to appoint Bernard Browne as General Secretary of the Labour Party is not only a public rebuke to the trade union movement, but further consolidates the party's image as a mere appendage to the Fine Gael Parliamentary Party," said the letter.

"The Party's leadership has been inexplicable ... The month long campaign against the unanimous recommendation showed contempt for Labour's internal decision process and public credibility."

The controversy did little for the party's public image.

"The contest had long taken on the limped-legged characteristics of Ireland's search for a soccer manager, as reports of the changing advantage to contenders for the job re-inforced the cliché of an organisation that is firmly determined to be an amateur," wrote Maire Crowe, a reporter with the *Irish Press*.

Kavanagh quickly identified himself with the party mainstream, and far away from the anti-coalitionists. His main claim to fame was that he had acted as national director for the anti-amendment campaign in 1983.

Reporter Crowe compared him to singer Bing Crosby in being able to go straight down the middle. He could "even be more polite than Dick Spring" when discussing the Militant Tendency, she added.

In June 1986 a bombshell hit the Labour Party when former chairman and Junior Minister Joe Bermingham resigned, a move that caused the Coalition Government to lose its overall majority. But there was no immediate threat to the Government.

Central to Deputy Bermingham's decision was the candidature of his one-time close associate, Emmet Stagg, a noted anti-coalitionist to replace him on the Labour ticket.

Bermingham had favoured Senator Timmy Conway, who had been nominated by the constituency convention, but this was not ratified by the party. Senator Conway subsequently joined the Progressive Democrats.

Three local Kildare councillors also resigned with Deputy Bermingham.

A statement claimed the county had no real say over its affairs.

"We were taken over by head office and the Administrative Council which is the party's ruling body, who effectively silenced us by directing that we should not hold constituency meetings, or issue statements. Then they even refused to ratify our choice of candidate to replace Joe Bermingham."

Ironically, Kildare was the constituency represented for over 30 years by a previous party leader, William Norton.

Bermingham was one of those who had persuaded Spring to take the leadership, but now he felt disillusioned.

"It's very hard to assess Dick Spring, because it is very hard to know Dick Spring," he told the *Irish Press* at the time. "He never really got to grips with what it takes to operate as leader. He doesn't open up with people.

"I was always worried about his lack of communication with the back-benchers and I don't think he can put passion into his efforts to convince people, like Corish, Cluskey or even O'Leary."

The Kildare man claimed that the 1973-77 Coalition had much more to show for its efforts.

He was wary, too, of Garret FitzGerald from his days as Minister in the Office of Public Works:

"Garret gets carried away with bullshit... There is this thing, preserving Bewley's, sure, Jaysus, that's nonsense. You might as well preserve the Gem in Naas if they were broke. It's only a coffee shop. That shows the weak side of him."

Bermingham was fearful of how Spring would fare at the autumn conference in Cork where the Electoral Strategy Commission report was due to be considered.

Former Labour deputy Seán Treacy, who had favoured Frank Cluskey rather than Spring for the leadership in 1982, was scathing of Spring in August of 1986.

"Dick Spring has an awful lot to answer for," he told Gerald Barry of the *Sunday Tribune*. "What is the latest poll? 4 per cent? My God! From any standpoint his leadership has been disastrous."

"I cannot understand it," continued Treacy, "I got on well with his father. But Dan went to National School and the Christian Brothers. He (Dick) went to Trinity College, the house of the ascendancy classes in this country. Maybe that's the difference."

One of Labour's weaknesses during its Coalition period was its failure, like all other political parties, to attract more women. In 1985 there were only five women among the 45-strong Administrative Council. There were just three women in the Parliamentary Party, Senators Helena McAuliffe-Ennis, Mary Robinson and Deputy Eileen Desmond. (Robinson left at the end of 1985, and McAuliffe-Ennis joined the PDs for a time.) Eileen Desmond was only the second woman in the history of the State (Maire Geoghegan-Quinn was the first) to be appointed to the Cabinet since the signing of the Treaty.

But already active in the background of the party were future Ministers Niamh Bhreathnach and Eithne Fitzgerald.

"Sometimes when I've been working with a child," said Bhreathnach, a teacher of mildly mentally handicapped children, in 1985, "I can see an improvement internally, but it takes a while for the school to register just how much the child has improved. It's a bit like that with the Labour Party."

The autumn of 1986 saw the focus of attention within Labour switch to the report of the Commission on Electoral Strategy. The Commission had been set up by a resolution for the Party's Annual Conference in Cork in 1985.

It had a broad range of aims, but yet again, all attention focused on its recommendations on future Coalition strategy.

The Commission was comprised of 22 members, including party Leader Dick Spring, Michael D Higgins, Peter Cassells, Bill Attley, Niamh Bhreathnach, Mervyn Taylor and General Secretary Ray Kavanagh. The chairman was Niall Greene, an executive with Guinness Peat Aviation, and a former chief executive of the Youth Employment Agency.

The group held 17 sessions throughout 1985 and 1986. Dick Spring attended seven of the meetings.

During the deliberations, Spring and Barry Desmond were anxious to avoid a decision to categorically rule out participation in Government for the rest of the century.

But the Leader made it clear that he was not anxious to participate in Government after the 1987 election even if Labour held the balance of power. But he was set against a decision to rule out *any* possibility of Coalition.

In the end, the Commission recommended that the party fight all elections on an independent basis and stay out of power for a period of ten to fifteen years.

"Our medium term goal over ten to fifteen years must be to restore the party vote to its previous levels and to exceed its best past performances," said the report. It continued:

"This requires that the party fight all elections on the basis of its independent policies and remain independent of all Governments, save in those circumstances where National Conference decides that exceptional national concerns dictate otherwise in order to defend the vital interests of our own electorate."

The conclusions were a reasonable compromise. Labour would remain independent for the foreseeable future, but the door was not entirely closed on the idea of Coalition.

But the report, adopted at the Annual Conference, placed further strains on an already divided Coalition Government. An editorial in the *Sunday Tribune* in August 1986 said: "There are persuasive reasons for arguing that Labour should stand aside from government for a period of perhaps up to 20 years to redefine its own identity and to recover the electoral ground that has been forfeited in the last decade and a half."

12
LABOUR AND LAZARUS

Late on election count night in February 1987 in Tralee, a journalist with the *Kerryman* newspaper, Tim Vaughan, approached the leader of the Labour Party. He was desperate to get some comment from Dick Spring as his paper was going to print early the following morning.

"Mr Spring," the reporter pleaded, "can I have reaction to your poor showing in the count?"

"Would you fuck off," roared an indignant Spring, now visibly angry at the way things were shaping up.

Vaughan was furious when, a few minutes later, he saw Mr Spring go upstairs to do a live interview with RTE television.

Vaughan (now deputy night news editor with *The Cork Examiner*) had been working with the *Kerryman* for only a short time, but had met Dick Spring on a walkabout during the election campaign. His exchanges with Spring had been pleasant and he was taken aback at the Labour Leader's reaction to a relatively innocuous question.

It wasn't the first time Dick Spring was shown to have a short fuse with his local newspaper. His relationship with the paper, owned by the Independent Group, was always tense.

In 1977 at the election count for his father, Dan, tempers had flared as he nearly lost his seat.

Then a photographer, working for the *Kerryman,* got too close for Dick's comfort. The dynamic sportsman, just married and back from New York, threatened the photographer that he would "wrap the camera round his neck" if he did not get it out of his way quickly. The photographer duly obliged, but was taken aback by the high temper.

In 1979 when Spring was picked for the Irish rugby team, the *Kerryman* didn't mention the fact. They just didn't think it was of any interest.

"At the time it was like being picked to play tiddlywinks," said one commentator.

During the abortion debate in 1983 Spring was extremely annoyed at a piece in the *Kerryman* headed "Is Spring an abortionist?".

Rather than ring the editor, Séamus McConville, Spring first tried to contact the paper's proprietor, Dr Tony O'Reilly, in Pittsburgh, USA. He failed to contact O'Reilly, but managed to talk to the managing director of Independent Newspapers in Dublin, Bartle Pitcher.

Spring managed to delay publication of the Tralee edition until he was given a right of reply underneath the "offending" article.

Only later did McConville, "over the passage of time", come to hear of Spring's attempts to phone Pittsburgh.

Fences seemed to be mended again in August 1983 when Spring gave his abortion amendment "Vote No" statement to the local paper in advance of all the national media.

But he ran into another squall on the eve of his departure for the Chequers meeting with Mrs Thatcher.

Spring told the *Kerryman* that the Chequers meeting would aim to restore Anglo-Irish relations following the "damage" done by Haughey's Falklands stance. But the Tánaiste refused to elaborate on how he saw Mr Haughey's decision not to support sanctions against Argentina as the wrong decision.

The *Kerryman* defied Spring and printed that he would not respond to their queries, and the atmosphere became icy once more.

But his waspish sense of humour has broken out in his dealings with the newspaper.

In October 1992 the advertising manager of the *Kerryman*, Brendan Doran, sent out a circular to all public representatives, in which he pointed out that the paper had "91 per cent penetration in Kerry".

In due course Dick Spring sent in his clinics' advertisement, accompanied by a note which read:

"I herewith attach a listing of clinics for this week's *Kerryman*. I sincerely hope that the 83,000 adults (91 per cent penetration in Kerry) do not turn up to my clinics! I would also be interested to find out who the remaining 9 per cent are? Regards, Dick Spring TD."

In his early election campaigns, Spring would come in and tour the *Kerryman*, shaking hands with all the workforce. Indeed many of the 60-strong team that produce the paper are loyal supporters.

But in recent campaigns he has neglected to visit the paper at all, which is located in Clash Industrial Estate, on the outskirts of the town.

The current editor, Brian Looney, has a good, working relationship with Dick Spring. They meet mostly on formal occasions in the town, or at weekend sporting events, when Spring likes to relax with his young sons, Aaron and Adam.

"Good afternoon, Mr Editor," Spring glibly greeted Looney once at a Saturday afternoon rugby match in the town in 1992.

"Good afternoon, former deputy prime minister," retorted Looney instantly, determined to meet "formal with formal".

But the two have the occasional pint together and their relationship is described as "good".

****

The 1987 election was extremely difficult for Dick Spring. During the campaign he said the onus was on people who had been knocking the party from within during its period of Government to now work harder.

"I'm leading a Left-wing party," he declared. "I want to take over democratic Left-wing politics in this country and I'll be saying: 'Now fellas, are you prepared to do the foot-slogging?'."

At all times he insisted that the party would not be entering Government, in accordance with the report of the 1986 Commission.

He rightly predicted that Fianna Fáil would not win an overall majority, and that Fine Gael and the PDs would not have enough votes for a majority either.

After leaving Government, political observers reckoned that Dick Spring was one of the few Labour deputies certain to make it back to the 25th Dáil. Furthermore, Fine Gael had put in a terrific campaign to get Senator Jimmy Deenihan elected in the constituency, having missed out by only 144 votes in November 1982.

Prior to the election, Fine Gael had come up with the idea of a quiz, based on their candidate Deenihan. Thousands of households were circulated with a questionnaire on Deenihan's sporting achievements. Over 5,000 replies were received as young people competed for valuable prizes of BMX bicycles which were a craze at the time.

Appointed to the Seanad by Garret FitzGerald, Deenihan had worked diligently in the constituency throughout the four years and frequently was the one to announce good news of various schemes.

When the count got under way it immediately appeared that there had been a huge fall-off in Spring's vote. Nationally the vote

was way down on 1982, and for a time it looked as though Dick Spring would lose his own seat, a huge embarrassment for the outgoing Tánaiste and Minister for Energy.

"It was a nightmare evening for Spring as he watched his top of the poll position in the last election slashed by Fine Gael's Jimmy Deenihan," wrote *Irish Times* reporter Joe Carroll. "At one stage the anti-Coalition tide threatened to wipe out half the party's 13 outgoing seats."

In Dublin, former leader Frank Cluskey was at one stage declared elected, but then deemed not elected following a Fianna Fáil objection. However, he was confirmed elected on a re-count.

Deenihan topped the poll and was elected on the first count with 10,087 votes. Spring with 6,737 was fighting for the last seat with long-standing FF TD Tom McEllistrim. When the surplus votes of elected Fianna Fáil deputy Denis Foley were distributed, they were not enough to bring his running mate above Spring, who was elected on the sixth count without reaching the quota.

On that night the McEllistrim Dáil record of unbroken service for 64 years was finally broken. The Spring Dáil record of 43 years unbroken service continued. But the drop in Labour support in North Kerry was only exceeded in Meath and in South Tipperary (where Seán Treacy had become an Independent deputy). At 6.4 per cent, the party was at its lowest ever point in the polls.

During the campaign Spring had again distanced himself from any Coalition with Fianna Fáil when he said the "party had become stultified in the grip of one man".

In a speech to party workers in Tralee, he re-asserted his old hostility to Haughey:

"Fianna Fáil's spokesmen increasingly look and sound like the dog on the old record labels who sat listening to his master's voice coming from the speaker."

The PDs also made a major breakthrough in this election with 16 seats, which led to a high deal of tension when the Dáil met for the first time. (Fianna Fáil, with 81 seats, was still short two for an overall majority).

Seán Treacy, who had been Ceann Comhairle in the 1973-77 Coalition was re-elected to the chair. But the outcome of the election of Charles Haughey depended on the votes of Independents Neil Blaney and Tony Gregory. Blaney supported Haughey, but Gregory abstained, leading to a tied vote of 82/82. Treacy then exercised his casting vote in favour of Haughey, who was elected Taoiseach. Garret FitzGerald was finally out of office.

Dick Spring was now the Leader of a party with only 12 deputies (he had predicted between 14 and 18 seats before the election), but the Parliamentary Party had a new look.

Gone were some of the older, more conservative deputies, including John Ryan in North Tipperary, Michael Moynihan in South Kerry, Joe Bermingham in Kildare and Frank Prendergast in Limerick East.

Back came Michael D Higgins in Galway West, and in came Emmet Stagg in Kildare and Brendan Howlin in Wexford, regaining the traditional Labour seat there, long held by Brendan Corish.

Spring's own poor personal showing led to questions being raised about his continued leadership of the party. He took off on a lengthy holiday to the United States and there were reports that he might never come back.

He admitted it had been a "harrowing campaign" and that his warning that there are no safe Labour seats had been borne out. In his own situation he said that he "had all to play for in the re-count, but it was like playing against the wind in both halves".

"The fact that Labour and Lazarus share an initial has been made agonisingly clear to its supporters by the events of the election count," wrote John Horgan in *The Irish Times.*

Horgan pointed out that the most obvious lesson from the fall-out was a distinct move to the Left. Up to that time the dominance of the conservative elements ensured there was no split, because if there was, it was the Left which would lose out.

Now the electorate had begun the task of rebuilding the party on the Left.

Strengthening its independence also meant that the party would not get its traditional transfers from Fine Gael, and this had serious implications for the future.

In his analysis, Horgan pointed out that one of the strange ironies about Labour and Fine Gael was that their differences surfaced more dramatically when they were in Government than when they were in Opposition. Spring would have to set about changing that in Opposition. This time he would also have to compete with the "glitterati" among the Progressive Democrats.

Then there was the growing problem of The Workers' Party, which now had four Dáil seats.

While well-meaning people thought unity on the Left was desirable, older, wiser heads knew that two parties competing for broadly the same electorate were unlikely to greet each other like long-lost brothers.

The theme of the 1987 Annual Conference in Cork City Hall was "Fighting for Your Future". And Dick Spring was indeed fighting for his. The conference was dominated by new proposals on how the Leader might be elected by the entire party participating.

Under the system, candidates would have had to secure nominations from two of the 17 trade unions affiliated to Labour, two TDs and two constituency councils.

Spring was totally opposed as it would give the unions a veto while he would have had to spend the next 12 months campaigning for the leadership, instead of building up the party.

So bruised was Spring by near-defeats that at one point he walked down from the platform, picked up the delegates' microphone, lost his temper yet again, and shouted: "I'm not taking this any more."

Spring and his supporters viewed the move, not as an extension of democracy, but as a preparation of the ground for a Left-wing bid on the leadership. Michael D would be first, would lose or be gobbled up by the real challenger, Emmet Stagg.

What was eventually agreed was to ask for a set of implications on how the system might operate to be brought before the next annual conference.

Among those most opposed to Spring in the debate were Higgins and Stagg.

Four deputies, one-third of the Party's Dáil strength, voted for the idea of conference voting every third year on the Leader. These were Emmet Stagg, Mervyn Taylor, Michael D Higgins and Michael Bell.

On a show of delegates cards, Deputy Higgins declared "carried" a proposition that a commission produce a report within a year on how and when the overall membership might elect a Leader.

Journalist Gerald Barry reported one associate of Emmet Stagg saying it would take a year, but "they would get Spring".

Within a few months of his election Emmet Stagg had emerged as the real threat to Dick Spring. The idea that Spring would always be succeeded by Michael D had diminished.

Down in Kildare, Stagg had built up a powerful political machine. He had more than 100 delegates at the conference in Cork out of a total of 1,200. It was the sort of support that could be bussed in from no other constituency, with the notable exception of North Kerry.

Relations between Spring and Stagg had always been tetchy.

At a Christmas party in 1986 the tension had erupted into open hostility when Spring lost his temper and confronted Stagg's Director of Elections in Kildare, David Moynan.

Eventually the ever-diplomatic Stagg separated them. The incident led to further bad feeling. Meanwhile, according to a report in *Phoenix* magazine at the time, Moynan's pullover had become something of a collector's item among the party faithful!

Then aged 43, Stagg was said to work for up to 120 hours a week. He had emerged in a short time as the biggest threat to the party establishment.

Not short of enemies, he also had a talent for winning friends and influencing people. He was effectively doing what Charles Haughey had done a decade previously, travelling the country and courting the grassroots.

While his critics claimed he would "leap into a Ministerial Merc if it pulled up at his door", he insisted that Labour should stay out of power until it was the majority partner in Government.

Before the conference, Spring had accused Stagg of "having a bee in his bonnet about my leadership".

In contrast to the Spring supporters, Stagg described the 1987 conference as "very positive, not at all negative".

Stagg, who was elected vice-chairman, denied that the conference was a submerged attack on Spring's leadership. However, he admitted that he would not support Spring for Leader.

"If I get the opportunity to vote for Michael D Higgins as Leader, I will do so – and have done so," he said, referring to his nomination of Higgins for the leadership at the first Parliamentary Party meeting after the previous election.

"The Vincent de Paul wing of the party and the socialist wing have co-operated before and will again," he added.

Dick Spring knew he had a fight on his hands.

"The stakes are high – the leadership itself," said one aide, "everything will have to be fought. But Dick has no shortage of bottle."

"A Leader who goes spare only when his own position is challenged has a great personal future," wrote Anne Harris in the *Sunday Independent*. "Look at Charles Haughey.

"Dick Spring has found anger late in life and he means to hold onto it, work on it and form a stable relationship with it.

"Dick Spring is the Leader of the Labour Party. The problem is there is nobody to lead. The Labour Party is now chasing a working class that votes Fianna Fáil and tells pollsters it admires Margaret Thatcher. From within, it is threatened by the Militant Left, from without by The Workers' Party and from above by its disenchanted paymasters, the trade union movement.

"All that Dick Spring has going for him right now is his anger. It might keep him in the leadership, but it won't put him in power."

13
DICK IS SUMMER, KRISTI IS WINTER

Dick Spring's moustache should go. It makes him look tired and drawn.

The message, delivered by Kerry woman Doreen Coleman to the Labour Leader in 1988 was not well received. Tidy it, yes, shorten it, maybe, but get rid of it altogether, definitely NO.

Doreen Coleman is a colour analyst, whose job it is to sharpen up people's presentation – get them to look smart, wear the correct colours to match their natural physique, that sort of thing.

"It's very important how you present yourself," says Doreen, "people do not realise that 60 per cent of attitude is based on first impressions. You have to present a total look, wear the clothes that suit you."

Many people, says Doreen, particularly women, have a wardrobe full of clothes and yet have nothing to wear.

In November 1988 Doreen Coleman took both Dick and Kristi Spring in hand. They agreed to go along with the "treatment". The results were published in the *Kerryman* newspaper.

Dick was naturally a little apprehensive at first.

"I suppose it was the thought of sitting still for so long!" he commented. But he was delighted with the results.

Doreen Coleman found that the Labour Leader belongs to the "summer" category. Warm colours suit him best, soft pinks, greens, and browns in particular.

"The choice of clothes available to a man in this country is limited," said Dick. "Either you wear a blue or a grey suit, or occasionally you try to break out of that by wearing a sports jacket."

Doreen recommended that he "tone things down a little, wear softer colours."

But Dick Spring drew the line at his moustache.

"I don't want to shave it off, I haven't a notion of it. I've had it nearly all my life and it's part of me. I started growing it in boarding school and they asked me to shave it off."

"Physically, Dick Spring could be described as classically handsome," wrote journalist Justine McCarthy in the *Irish Independent*. "But then there is the moustache, which no image-maker could condone. It has the effect of ageing him beyond his years, but he remains unconcerned."

According to Doreen Coleman, the moustache does not suit the business man image.

"I think beards and 'taches are more for the artistic types; it doesn't really go with the business image," she said, "but it does break the length of his face."

Kristi had mixed feelings about it.

"I like it but then I've never seen him without it, so I don't know how he'd look if he shaved it off," she said. "The cartoonists wouldn't like it anyway. Every time you see a cartoon of Dick, it's always the moustache that's exaggerated."

Both Kristi and Doreen also knocked glasses on the head for Dick.

"They make him look tired and drawn, particularly when he's on television. He should try out contact lenses," said Doreen. (Dick finally tried them for his Presidential address to the Labour Party conference in Waterford in 1993.)

For Kristi, Doreen Coleman concluded that she looked best in bold, striking colours like reds, royal blues and, particularly, black and white.

When off duty at home, Dick likes loafing about in jeans and a casual jacket.

Being out of Government from 1987 on gave Dick Spring a little more time to be with his family and to get some relaxation.

Shortly after Spring left Government, his son Aaron, then aged 5, came rushing into his father's bedroom, drummed him awake with his fists and squealed: "Daddy, do you live here again?"

Meetings and funerals are dread words with the children, Aaron (12), Laura Lee (10), and Adam (7).

His time with his family is limited, and mainly confined to weekends.

"It's not a normal life. It's unreal," he admits and makes it clear he knows the price he is paying.

"They won't come to me if they have a problem – they go to their mother. You cannot schedule your kids. You cannot say to them: 'I will see you on Saturday morning and we will talk about your problems.' Those problems will probably arise on Wednesday morning."

Since the car accident in December 1981 he has been compelled to give up all sports, except for a little golf and some therapeutic swimming.

While Tánaiste he attended up to 50 meetings of various kinds each week including one or two Cabinet meetings.

In 1986 he took up fishing, mainly as a result of pressure from his four-and-a-half-year-old son, Aaron, who had developed a passion for the sport.

"He's a great get-up-and-go man," said Dick, "probably because of his American blood. We Irish are poor at that sort of thing."

He remarked on the poor use of natural facilities by the Irish people.

"Down in Tralee we have those magnificent mountains, less than three miles from the centre of the town - but few people from the town ever bother with them.

"Now if Tralee were a town in Denmark or any of the Scandinavian countries, those mountains would be alive with people every weekend."

Dick Spring's lifestyle has meant that he is away from his

wife and family for a great part of each week.

In Dublin he lives in what he once described as "a most monastic flat", because very few had ever had a cup of tea there.

From there throughout the 1980s, he would emerge, two or three mornings each week, to swim in a nearby pool.

In Tralee he swims in the sports complex attached to the Mount Brandon Hotel.

"Swimming on your back is boring," he said. "It's all about strengthening the back muscles."

One advantage to him is that he has never had any weight problem and is superbly fit.

"When I was playing rugby I was always aiming at being 13 stone. The best I did was to get to 12 stone 8 pounds, and then, after the car crash, I went down to 10 stone."

He believes his sporting career helped him enormously.

"And it isn't only in fitness. You learn to take knocks, to pick yourself up and to get going again."

And he remembers the Cistercian monastery where he went to school.

"There was a very good atmosphere there. It was very relaxed, yet you had to do your work. And I learned something about organisation."

Spring has always been a light eater, too. Breakfast never consists of more than a slice of toast and a cup of tea. Then he will have either a good lunch or a good evening meal, but never both.

Dick Spring is a voracious reader, and has on occasions threatened to write himself.

"I kept a diary for a while," he revealed. "When I found myself in Berlin I felt I couldn't go through it without writing down my feelings. I want to sit down and make a record of my years in politics. I've kept notes and minutes of meetings."

Once he told how a much respected, older politician said to

him: "You should be keeping a record because you have to protect yourself in future."

Spring is also a good sleeper, no matter how great the pressures. He can drop off instantly, and can sleep in the car.

"Frequently I get two hours sleep between Tralee and Dublin," he adds.

"So far in my life nothing has ever succeeded in giving me a sleepless night. Once, when there was a re-count pending and my seat hanging in the balance I still managed to get a perfect night's sleep. That's very important to me. If ever I started to have sleepless nights, that, I think, would be the time to get out.

"Early in the morning is the time to get the work done. It is much easier to avoid the distractions then."

During the 1980s one of his ways of relaxing was to take a stroll after finishing work and drop into one of the pubs he frequented as a student. He rarely has any problems with "messers", and most people respect his privacy.

He has long learned to cope with crises, particularly during his first term as Tánaiste.

"Anyone who takes a job like that and thinks they can live a stress-free life is really living in cloud-cuckoo-land."

Sometimes he admits he flies off the handle. It is good to let off steam, he argues.

"Letting off steam occasionally doesn't do any harm. Do it too often and people will take no notice of you. But it isn't any harm that people should know there are limits to one's patience."

He once smoked a pipe, but has now given up smoking completely.

"I never smoked cigarettes, but I liked the pipe. Then I found myself getting very fond of cigars, so I quit."

Politics has meant that he still has to sit in a lot of smoke-filled rooms, but that's part of the job.

Spring is also a fan of American singer Bob Dylan. During the 1983-87 Coalition he wrote an article for *The Irish Times* about Dylan and had his photograph taken wearing a leather jacket. People were either horrified that a Tánaiste could wear such a thing, or delighted that the Leader of the Labour Party could smile.

Two of his favourite Dylan songs are "Blowin' in the Wind", and "The Times They are A'Changin", which he says best encapsulate both the freedom and the idealism of the 1960s.

"They spoke volumes to young people and to their worried parents – far more volumes than the more overtly rebellious forms of music."

Spring and Dylan parted company when the latter discovered electric rock music – about the same time as the former discovered politics.

The Labour Leader has also a mocking and a cynical sense of humour, which is usually kept well battened down in public.

"Dick Spring is a very private and rather defensive person whose idea of a conversation is a Socratic dialogue, with questions being deflected and answered as questions," wrote Joseph O'Malley, political correspondent of the *Sunday Independent*.

"His humour is sardonic and biting, a defence mechanism to conceal his own shyness, while the moustache adds an enigmatic quality to the distinctly Edwardian appearance."

But he finds it difficult to take criticism, and snarls in the Dáil when members of the Opposition criticise him or poke fun at him.

In the spring of 1993 while Fine Gael's Jim Higgins was berating Health Minister, Brendan Howlin, over his response to an alleged abuse case in the west of Ireland, Tánaiste Spring could be overheard muttering "bollocks" under his breath. Howlin simply demanded that Higgins withdraw his allegations.

By nature, Dick Spring is rather shy and retiring. On the election hustings he is not a baby-kisser. He has no great enthusiasm for the "grip and grin" back-slapping aspect of politics.

Colleagues say that while he is very courteous to, and attracted by women, he is never quite comfortable in their company. He is more relaxed when he is "with the lads".

Fine Gael colleague Jimmy Deenihan once described him as "the cutest politician in Dáil Éireann". He described Spring's cuteness as "keeping your cards very close to your chest, keeping people guessing and seizing opportune moments to make statements and at the same time knowing when not to make a statement".

As for the plámás and the glad handing, Spring says: "I prefer to be working rather than soft-soaping."

His North Kerry constituency is run very tightly.

Dick Spring's sister, Maeve, also a county councillor, gave up her civil service job some years ago to look after his constituency matters. She is a member of one of the four Labour branches in Tralee. Dick is a member of another, the Rock St branch, while his mother Anna, is in a third. The only branch outside their direct influence is largely controlled by another long-time councillor, Michael O'Regan.

Relations between O'Regan, who is blind, and Spring, have often been strained. Observers say that O'Regan, a totally committed party man, has never been allowed to advance in Kerry politics. He would, say observers, have been an ideal nominee to the Seanad, yet he was passed over while Albert Reynolds scored highly in nominating Brian Crowley from West Cork, who is confined to a wheelchair, to the Seanad in 1993. O'Regan has never even been "allowed" make it to Kerry County Council as Dick has always insisted on standing alone.

Most recently, in March 1993, when Dick resigned his county council seat on being appointed Tánaiste, O'Regan again failed to get the nomination, which went instead to a cousin of Spring's.

14

THE ALL-AMERICAN GIRL

In the mid-1950s in Richmond, Virginia, USA, a young girl named Kristi Lee Hutcheson was given a present of an Irish Setter dog.

Kristi had no Irish relations and knew nothing about Ireland. She had to look it up on the atlas to find out where it was. On the atlas she saw a place called "Kerry" and decided to give her dog the same name.

Kristi Hutcheson was the eldest of a family of six, who were members of the First Christian Church. Her mother is of German/Russian extraction and her father is a mixture of Italian, French and Scots. Her father was a designer in a shipyard and her mother was a nurse.

After early schooling, Kristi went on to study for a science degree in education and art at the Virginia Commonwealth University in Richmond.

"I was very happy growing up," she recalls. "I was among the first to be involved in the integration of the black and white communities in education. I studied for my Masters in Education and worked in a tough, black inner city school in remedial work."

Politics, especially the politics of another country, would have been fairly low on any list of subjects. Even after she turned 21, and was eligible to vote, she didn't consider herself very politically aware.

"I really wasn't that political, other than just voting. My family was never registered or anything. In fact my mother and father would often disagree and vote different ways. And I tended to vote more the way I thought and felt at the time about certain candidates."

If she was to categorise her politics then, she says she would have been Left of the Democratic Party.

She met Dick Spring while they were both on a career break in New York. At the time, in 1976, she had moved to New York to work as an air hostess with Trans America International, and was based in Manhattan.

The only member of the family to have a longing to travel, she had no plans whatever to marry and settle down – until she met a handsome barman, named Spring.

Dick was taking a few years break after qualifying for the Bar, and for a while had thought of taking up Law in the States.

Today, Dick Spring looks very different from the Dick Spring who first served her table in the Mad Hatter bar in New York.

"He had long curly hair, and mutton-chop side-burns. He had a Heathcliff look about him.

"There was something so different and unique about him. He had quiet self-confidence, without being obtrusive. He was soft-spoken but very articulate. And I liked the way he got on with so many people.

"He also had this air of romance, of something off the moors, that curly hair and the long moustache, yes, Edwardian."

They had been introduced by a mutual friend, Jerry, but did not become close friends for some months.

However, by the beginning of February 1977 they had decided to get married and did so in her home state of Virginia the following June.

Kristi knew that Dick intended to come back to Ireland, and in fact he left for Kerry the Monday after they got married to canvass for his father's re-election.

"I knew that his father was in politics and that obviously he had to come back after our wedding and that he felt strongly about that. But one cannot understand the political system here until you're in the middle of it."

When he met Kristi Hutcheson, Dick Spring confided three things in her. He wanted to practise at the Bar, win a rugby cap for Ireland and get elected to the Dáil.

The couple moved back to Dublin and rented a house in Blackrock.

The first year was "very rough", she later admitted.

"I was surprised that Dublin was quite a big city, although small enough to be a welcome relief from New York. The only thing that really bothered me was the rain. It was raining when I arrived and it didn't stop for the next three years. At least that's how it seemed at the time."

Although Dick was practising at the Bar and doing reasonably well, their income was "very meagre".

So Kristi went off and picked up the pieces of her original teaching career which she had left behind when she was hit by the travel bug to become an air hostess.

In Dublin she went to work at the Cluain Mhuire family centre at Blackrock run by the St John of God Brothers. There her specialist knowledge as a remedial teacher was put to work in remedial teaching and play therapy among disturbed children.

In 1979 Dick Spring was elected to both Tralee Urban District Council and Tralee County Council, and they moved down to Kerry. Kristi found it all mesmerising.

Dick's Dáil aspirations were almost knocked at the first outing, and Kristi can still recall the "long count" in June 1981 when the Spring seat looked in serious danger.

"Dick and I went down to the hall that night prepared to concede victory as Ger Lynch of Fine Gael seemed to be winning. However, the tide changed and the transfers started to come in."

It was just four weeks after the birth of her first son, Aaron.

Life took on a new dimension when Dick Spring was made Minister of State for Justice on his first day in the Dáil. As her role model, she chose her mother-in-law, Anna Spring.

"I had watched how they (Dan and Anna) ran things and with Dick becoming a Junior Minister, we had to be organised from the very first day.

"Dick was spending a lot of time in Dublin so clinics had to be set up. In the long run that was better for us because I didn't have a lot of people coming to our door. But the phone was very demanding."

Then came the serious road accident in December1981 which was to have a permanent effect on their lives.

"I do not look at anything in my life as if it's going to last for years and years," she said at the time.

Her first solo test as a canvasser came in the November 1982 election while Dick was still recuperating in hospital.

"Before I went out," she recalled, "I didn't know how I'd be received. You know, being a Yank, if you like. Despite the fact that I was Dick Spring's wife, I was an outsider, but it only took one night of canvassing ... the people I met were wonderful. I felt they're just people and I was their messenger. I was Dick's wife and it was as if they said, 'If I was good enough for him, I was good enough for them'."

Kristi Spring did not see herself as a policy shaper in her husband's life, but rather as a support.

But her deepest reservation came in November 1982 when Michael O'Leary resigned as Leader of the party. The momentum of support for Dick Spring swelled immediately within the ranks of the party.

In one interview, she recalled that, on the Friday night before the leadership election Dick had come home to tell of the growing support for him from his party colleagues.

"We talked about it all the weekend. I had reservations about his youth, his relatively short time in the Dáil, and especially his health.

"However, as the calls of encouragement and support came in, I felt that his colleagues wanted him and my only worry was Dick's health. We went to see the consultant on the Saturday and Dick's back was checked out. He said Dick was ready to do this highly-demanding job."

Kristi is a much more private person than Dick and makes fewer close friendships.

But she faced through all the difficulties of adapting to living in Ireland, something that might have overcome a weaker character.

One of her first difficulties, for example, was religion.

She had been born into the First Christian Church which is along the lines of the Baptist Church, and grew up practising in the Baptist Church. But the Church of Ireland was as removed from her experience as the Catholic Church.

Their three children are being brought up as Catholics and Kristi goes to Mass with them and Dick.

She has also had to confront the issues of divorce and abortion, which were major topics of debate during Dick Spring's first term as Tánaiste.

In an interview in 1987 she said on abortion:

"Personally it would be anathema to me. I couldn't imagine wanting it. But it is one thing to say I don't want it, and another to pressurise people in very, very different circumstances and say 'what I don't want, you can't have'."

On women's position in Ireland she also found some odd practices. She was horrified, when at the age of 26, she was turned down for a job on age grounds. That, she said, would never have happened in the States.

As Dick is away so much of the time, Kristi Spring pursues her own interests during the week. She loves hill-walking and swimming. The water, she says, is a natural environment and people should make more use of it.

Dick Spring had never learned to swim as a child. Kristi's parents couldn't either, but they were determined that their children would. Kristi loved it and was pretty good on her team in Virginia.

But she is also happy in her own company.

Sewing, cross-stitch embroidery, and pottery take up some of her time.

When she first arrived she was amazed at the Irish humour. But now that she's been here for 16 years, she feels she's more in the picture. She describes Kerry humour as "cute and clever. They leave a lot unsaid."

Kristi has maintained her own independence. This is most exemplified by the fact that she has never forsaken her American citizenship. As a result she cannot vote for her husband.

"Being an American is what I am and I'm very proud of that. I was 26 when I came to Ireland, so I had lived a much longer time in America."

She still makes frequent trips home, either with the children or with Dick.

"It's a great breather – you can really let your hair down with your own family."

Furthermore, in America Dick Spring can be completely anonymous.

In the recent American presidential election, Kristi thought it was time for change. She is also impressed by Hillary Clinton and is interested in observing how she will cope in the White House.

These days she tries to ensure that Dick gets plenty of time with his children, as it is a time they will remember. As their time together as a family is precious, they usually spend it at home on the outskirts of Tralee. Spring has often admitted that his situation is saved by the fact that he married Kristi, "a strong American lady".

She is happy that the children have coped well so far, and at the last general election she had to restrain them from going out canvassing. Already young Aaron has expressed an interest in getting into politics and in continuing on the family dynasty.

"It's something that seems to get into the blood system," said Kristi.

15
MILITANT TENDENCY

Dick Spring's image as the real Leader of the Opposition was given a major boost on 2 September 1987.

On that day the new Fine Gael Leader, Alan Dukes, launched the Tallaght Strategy, a new system of parliamentary politics whereby his party supported the minority Fianna Fáil Government as long as it pursued "responsible" economic policies. The announcement caused some astonishment in Fine Gael and Labour and, indeed, within Fianna Fáil circles.

The move led to the business of the Dáil being agreed between the Government and Fine Gael whips each week, with Labour left to get angry and complain, but unable to do much else. Fine Gael managed, with the agreement of the Government, to dominate Private Members' Time, while Labour and the Progressive Democrats lost out.

At all times Fine Gael had to avoid getting the agreement of all the Opposition parties on any of their motions, because if they did, then the Government would be defeated. And that was the last thing Alan Dukes wanted.

The usual procedure was to put in an amendment to any Labour motion, advocating privatisation or some other clause, which would be unacceptable to them. This ensured the Government's survival.

However, at the end of November the Government was defeated on a motion concerning education cuts when there was lack of communication between the Taoiseach, Charles Haughey, and his Education Minister, Mary O'Rourke.

There was a second defeat for the Government during Private Members' Time at the end of the year over extra funding for the National Social Services Board.

Before Christmas 1988 the Taoiseach had a lengthy meeting with Alan Dukes at which they agreed there would be no general election until the end of 1989 at the earliest. It was a remarkable development in Irish political life.

Meanwhile, Labour Leader Dick Spring was fast finding his feet as Leader of a Party in Opposition although his Dáil manoeuvrings were severely limited by the sweetheart deal between Fianna Fáil and Fine Gael.

Time and again Spring knocked any notion of a future Coalition with Fianna Fáil.

"There are some who describe themselves as being on the Left in Irish politics who argue that it is both desirable and necessary to persuade Fianna Fáil to move to the Left, and who would be interested in supporting a Fianna Fáil Government that offered Left wing policies," he told a meeting of North Tipperary constituency on 21 April 1988.

"This is a naïve and silly point of view. The record of Fianna Fáil in the past ten years, ever since 1977, is a record of a party that is totally unscrupulous. Their every action, and especially their every promise, is geared towards one objective only – the retention of power for themselves.

"My advice to anyone gullible enough to think that Fianna Fáil can be genuinely turned to the Left is to think again. If we want Left-wing politics in Ireland, we have to build it from the ground up. Fianna Fáil, if it suits them, will wear Left-wing clothes for a while, but a wolf in sheep's clothing is still a wolf."

By the early months of 1989 Dick Spring was preparing for yet another difficult annual conference, but the bonus was that the venue was in his own home constituency, in Tralee. This guaranteed him plenty of friendly Kerry faces among the delegates.

But the conference opened with a hiccup for Spring – or rather a punch-up!

The previous week he had become embroiled in an incident with John Cooney, then a feature columnist with *The Irish Times*.

During a discussion in the Visitors' bar of Dáil Éireann involving SDLP Leader John Hume and RTE journalist Rodney Rice, Cooney invited Spring to speak at the General Humbert Summer School, of which he was the director. Spring took out his diary and mockingly told Cooney that he had a much more important date at the Puck Fair in Kerry. Cooney laughed at this put-down, and said his invitation was serious.

Again, Spring was flippant in his response suggesting that if need be, he would stay on the other side of the Atlantic Ocean to avoid a sojourn in Mayo. Cooney felt mortified in front of Hume and Rice.

"I enjoyed the Puck Fair apologia," Cooney recalls. "But when I gave Dick a second serve, I did expect a serious response. His further put-down was out of court as far as I was concerned."

Later Cooney approached Spring in a Dáil corridor and called him a "shit". Spring was incensed, took off Cooney's glasses and slapped him on the face.

The following morning Spring contacted the editor of *The Irish Times*, Conor Brady, to lodge a complaint. (Spring and Brady had both attended Mount St Joseph's in Roscrea.) This representation was conveyed to Cooney later that day by Ken Gray, the then managing editor, and Cooney was summoned to his office to explain his actions.

Cooney admitted that he had been involved in an incident with Spring, but when told by Gray that Spring was demanding an apology, he told *The Irish Times* number two executive "you must be joking".

Cooney told Gray that he was sorry for calling Spring a "shit" but he felt that he had been provoked by Spring's arrogant attitude. But the main point was that Spring had hit Cooney, not the other way round.

Gray, recognising the legal implications of the Cooney/Spring row, was prepared to allow time for the matter to settle, and Cooney returned to his desk to compile his Saturday column.

"I phoned Spring to clear up the matter, but Fergus Finlay would not put me through until I gave him an assurance that I was not about to assail 'the Party Leader'. When I got through to Dick, I immediately said I was sorry about our previous night's misadventure and we should clear it up. Dick was frosty and demanded an apology in writing. I was flabbergasted and told him so. But he said that he wanted the apology in writing to put it in a filing cabinet for use if I stepped out of line again. I said 'OK Dick, if that's the way you want it.'

"I wrote out a letter of apology saying 'Dear Dick, I apologise for calling you a 'shit.' I also forgive you for stealing my glasses and slapping my face'."

"I received an apology from Mr Cooney – albeit a snide apology, but I'm happy to leave the matter rest," Spring told the *Kerryman*.

The report under the headline "Dick Hits Journalist" was the lead story on the *Kerryman* on the day the Annual Conference opened in Tralee.

At his last conference in Cork, Dick Spring had had a rough time. Amid the backbiting, the rifts and the recriminations, a motion by the Left which could have ended his leadership of the party, had been narrowly defeated.

By March 1989 that particular bogey had subsided, as it looked certain that a report prepared by a commission would recommend that in future the Leader be elected by all the party.

But there were still a number of serious problems outstanding, notably that of the Militant Tendency.

The Militant organisation had its origins in Trotsky's days

and in some countries had existed as a separate political entity. However, in both Britain and Ireland it had tended to attach itself to the Labour Party and to secure a major influence.

British Labour MP, Shirley Williams, had once described its followers as "termites burrowing their way towards the heart of the party".

Former Labour Party TD, John Horgan, a staunch anti-Militant, described their designs as aimed at discrediting democratic socialism and to win converts for insurrectionary politics. They attempted to seep through the Labour Party like ink through blotting paper, he claimed.

In 1985, for example, its newspaper *Militant Irish Monthly* demanded that the Labour Party then in Government, and the "right-wing leaders who prop it up must be propelled from government".

"They are characterised," wrote Horgan, "not alone by their ideology, but by a peculiar manner of addressing public meetings, the words delivered in a monotone, accompanied by a robot-like chopping motion of the right hand. This appears to have been borrowed in part from the style of Ted Grant, the English leader of the tendency."

In the late 1980s the movement's principal convener in the Republic was Joe Higgins, a very affable man, and also a Kerryman, who is a fluent Irish speaker.

Higgins had given up his job as a teacher to work full-time for the organisation. He was an elected member of the Labour Party's Administrative Council.

Militants had long been a source of concern to the Labour Party leadership.

Brendan Halligan, as party General Secretary, had collected a lot of material on the organisation, while Frank Cluskey, during his leadership, had suggested that an investigation be carried out into their operations.

But it was Dick Spring who took the strongest stand against

the organisation which had major influence over Labour Youth. He had proposed that an investigation be carried out to see whether it infringed the Labour Party's constitution which specified that a member of the party could not be a member of any other political party "or of an organisation ancillary thereto". However, the investigation never took place.

Labour politicians like Michael D Higgins and Emmet Stagg, while never members of Militant, were opposed to the idea of expelling the Militants and, by the late 1980s, the issue had become a very thorny one for the party Leader, Dick Spring. It was, in effect, another test of the strength of his leadership.

Spring had always taken a hard line on the Militants, seeing them as a distraction and a hindrance to building up the Labour Party.

"I am determined that the Militant Tendency will not deter us from building up the party," he said in 1985. "They are a distraction and have nothing to contribute.

"They have decided not to force the issue and to an extent we have not forced it either. Dealing with the Milis is a bit like chasing the rainbow – the Milis don't exist, yet they're everywhere."

Back in Opposition, and with more time to attend to party matters, Spring was determined to finally sort out the Militants. In 1987, for example, the Dublin West constituency convention defied the instructions of the party's Organisation Committee and picked two candidates, Joe Higgins and Eamonn Tuffey. This alarmed Spring because it showed that Militants from around the country had gravitated to Dublin West to ensure Higgins would have the maximum convention vote.

A special investigation failed to prove anything concrete, yet it highlighted a growing problem.

At the last Conference in Cork the Tendency were able to control an estimated 125 votes and had carried the balance in such

Classmates at Tralee National School.
Front (l-r): Pat Lyne, Richie Boylan, Willie O'Connor. Second Row: Billy Ryle, Gerald Carey, Noel McCarthy, Tommy Sweeney, Maurice Barrett. Back Row: Timmy Sheehan, Tom O'Halloran, Francie McSwiney, Niall O'Neill, Jimmy Flynn, Richard Spring.

Austin Stacks – County Minor Hurling Champions 1967.
Front (l-r): J. Reidy, T. Sheehan, R. Spring, J. Power, J. Diggins, J. Dennehy, J. O'Callaghan, T. Kennington. Second Row: J. Reidy (selector, RIP), T. Hannifin, P. McCarthy, W. Ryle, A. O'Keeffe, J. Parker and J. Hobbert. Third Row: G. O'Keeffe, J. Crean, J. O'Keeffe, M. McCarthy (captain), J. Lenihan, M. Barry.

New rugby cap Dick Spring in Lansdowne Road on January 7, 1979.
Photo: Irish Press Library

Dick Spring, No. 15, an unsafe pair of hands?

Coming in to support the full-back are wing forward Colm Tucker and No. 8 Mike Gibson, while Colin Patterson looks on.

Attending his first Kerry Council meeting on 21 June 1979. From left: James Courtney (Ind.), Mick O'Connell (Ind.), Robert Beasley (Sinn Féin), Michael Moynihan (Lab.) and Dick Spring. Photo: Kevin Coleman/Kerryman.

The wrecked State Mercedes which crashed outside Nenagh on the morning of 15 December 1981. Dick Spring, the Junior Minister for Justice, was trapped in the wreckage for twenty minutes before being cut free by firemen. Photo: John Long/Nenagh Guardian.

Speaking in Tralee during the February 1982 general election with the Labour Party Leader, Michael O'Leary, and Dick's mother, Anna Spring. Photo: Kevin Coleman/Kerryman.

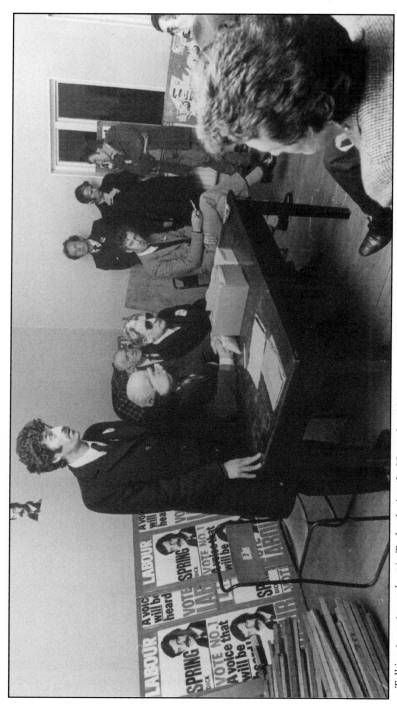

Talking to party workers in Tralee during the November 1982 general election. Seated on the far right is his brother, Dr Arthur Spring.
Photo: Kevin Coleman/The Kerryman.

Arriving with his wife Kristi for the first Dáil sitting after the February 1982 general election. Photo: Irish Press Library.

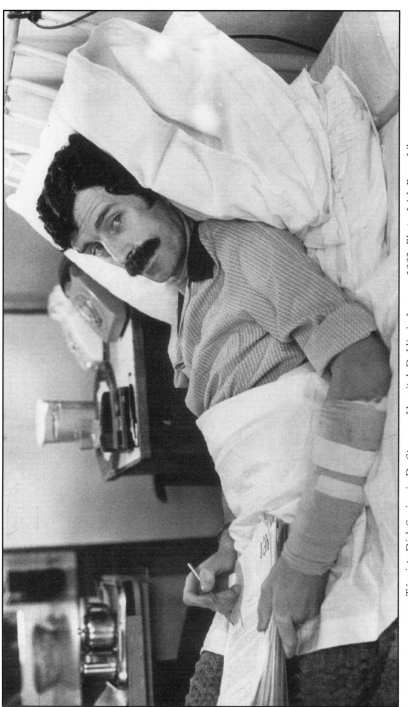

Tánaiste Dick Spring in Dr Steevens Hospital, Dublin in January 1983. Photo: Irish Press Library.

Tánaiste, Dick Spring, meets SDLP Leader John Hume outside Leinster House in 1993.
Photo: Eamonn Farrell/Photocall.

Tánaiste and Minister for Energy, Dick Spring, switches on natural gas in the home of Mrs Mary Dennehy in Walkinstown, Dublin, in May 1984. Also in the picture: Donal McAleese, Chief Executive, Dublin Gas and Dublin Lord Mayor, Michael Keating. Photo: Irish Press

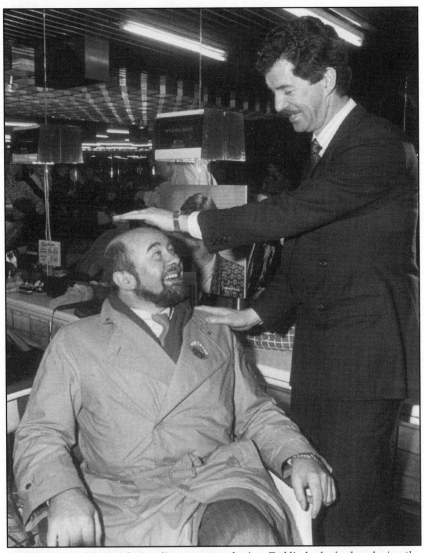

Dick Spring and Ruairí Quinn discuss new styles in a Dublin barber's shop during the 1987 general election. Photo: Irish Press Library.

Emmet Stagg, who threatened Dick Spring's leadership of the Labour Party in the 1980s and is now a Minister of State at the Department of the Environment. Photo: Eamonn Farrell/Photocall.

Outspoken Labour deputy for Sligo/Leitrim, Declan Bree.
Photo: Eamonn Farrell/Photocall.

With the British Labour Party leader, Neil Kinnock and Tipperary hurling captain, Declan Carr, outside the Burlington Hotel on the eve of the 1989 All-Ireland Final. Photo: Irish Press Library.

Dick Spring, accompanied by his son, Aaron, arriving to vote in Tralee for the Maastricht referendum in June 1992. Photo: Kevin Coleman/The Kerryman.

Planning tactics – Barry Desmond, Dick Spring, Sinéaid Bruton (Assistant Press Officer) and Fergus Finlay during the November 1992 general election. Photo: Eamonn Farrell/Photocall.

Cavan/Monaghan Labour candidate Ann Gallagher keeps an eye on the Party Leader while he does a telephone interview during the November 1992 election campaign. Photo: The Irish Times.

Acknowledging the applause in the National Concert Hall on 10 January 1993. Photo: Eamonn Farrell/Photocall.

Leaving the Beef Tribunal in Dublin Castle with his brother, Donal Spring.
Photo: Leo Farrell/Photocall.

The five Party Leaders meet to agree a Ceann Comhairle on 14 December 1992. From left: Des O'Malley, John Bruton, Albert Reynolds, Dick Spring and Proinsias de Rossa.

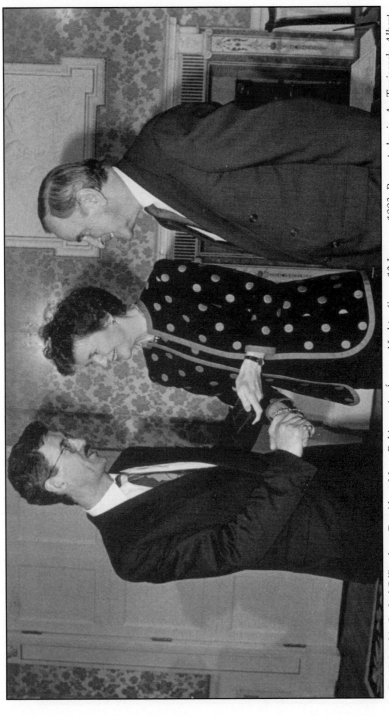

Receiving his Seal of Office from President Mary Robinson in Áras an Uachtaráin on 12 January 1993. Present also is An Taoiseach, Albert Reynolds. Photo: Eamonn Farrell/Photocall.

The January 1993 Cabinet. Photo: Eamonn Farrell/Photocall.

Seated (from left): Niamh Bhreathnach (Education), Maire Geoghegan-Quinn (Justice), Taoiseach Albert Reynolds, Tánaiste Dick Spring, Bertie Ahern (Finance). Standing: Michael D. Higgins (Arts, Culture and the Gaeltacht), Harry Whelehan (Attorney General), Brendan Howlin (Health), Ruairí Quinn (Enterprise and Employment), Michael Smith (Environment), Joe Walsh (Agriculture, Food and Forestry), Dr Michael Woods (Social Welfare), Mervyn Taylor (Equality and Law Reform), David Andrews (Defence and Marine), Brian Cowen (Transport, Energy and Communications), Charlie McCreevy (Trade and Tourism) and Noel Dempsey (Chief Whip).

Tánaiste and Minister for Foreign Affairs, Dick Spring, meeting Northern Ireland Secretary, Sir Patrick Mayhew, in Iveagh House on 22 January 1993. Photo: Eamonn Farrell/Photocall.

votes as the election of Mervyn Taylor as chairman over the head of Ruairí Quinn.

By the 1989 Conference in Tralee Spring had finally taken the decision to expel the Militants in the form of a motion on the programme.

In a pre-conference interview he said: "They (the Militants) are a separate organisation, they are a party within a party and you cannot be a member of both. It is certainly not in the best interest of the Labour Party. We are giving the people the option of belonging to one or the other – but you cannot belong to both."

Strict precautions on voting were taken at Tralee. The leadership believed that up to 40 delegates voted more than once at the Cork Conference in 1987 and were responsible for the election of one person to the Administrative Council.

Party bosses switched plans and marked the palms of delegates, after it became known that some were seeking a chemical solvent that would remove the indelible mark from the backs of their hands. But by putting the mark on the palms of delegates, double voting in the contests was virtually eliminated.

The crucial vote on expelling the Militants was carried by a margin of 86 votes. Spring's enormous delegation of 210 had a crucial influence on the outcome. The extreme Left was demolished and Dick Spring was in real control of the Labour Party.

"It was clear also that having put work into preparing the conference for a confrontation with the hard Left, Spring would not be persuaded, by late-hour offers of compromise from driving the sword through the throat," wrote John Foley of the *Irish Independent*.

In the end, the slaying of 500 Militants was accepted meekly but decisively, and without the dramatic conference-floor histrionics which were threatened.

The key vote had in fact taken place earlier in a private session when an appeal against the abolition of three Militant-controlled branches in Dublin West was defeated by 240 votes.

Spring was in control of the Labour Party by having cleared one of the major obstacles out of his way.

There were other victories for Spring in Tralee.

Niamh Bhreathnach, later appointed Minister for Education, defeated Emmet Stagg for the post of vice-chairperson, being elected with two votes to spare on the first count. The tables had been turned on Stagg, as the powerful ITGWU, among others, switched its vote. In 1987 Stagg had been elected vice-chairman with second count transfers from Joe Higgins of Militant Tendency.

A foul-up by Stagg's supporters also meant that Spring got clear control of the all-powerful Standing Orders Committee. The Committee has responsibility for ordering agenda business, and sets the rules for conference debates and procedures.

At the conference Spring had made clear his distaste for Emmet Stagg. Shortly before the party Leader spoke, Stagg had gone to the assistance of a speaker who could not get the microphone to work.

"I hope I'll get the mike working without assistance," quipped Spring as he rose to speak. Spring was king and nobody was going to de-throne him, especially in his own backyard.

The Tralee conference was also a watershed when the party introduced major changes in the traditional hour-long Leader's speech to the delegates on Saturday night, which was televised live by RTE.

To augment his script, Spring used a singer and an actor to good effect. He also employed the skills of two poets, WB Yeats and Dylan Thomas, by quoting verses from each.

The theme of the conference was "Bread and Roses" which was highlighted by Sharon Reddy's rendition of the song from which the theme was derived. The song commemorates a strike by woollen mill workers in 1912 in Massachusetts. It had been a bitter dispute and many of the women on the picket lines carried placards saying: "We want bread – and roses too."

In his speech, Spring turned to Dylan Thomas' poem "Do Not Go Gently Into That Good Night" for motifs of anger and rage in the face of a Government whose harsh policies, he said, were taken from the Lady of Downing Street.

And from Yeats' poem "Easter 1916" – read by actor Emmet Bergin – he used the line, "Too long a sacrifice can make a stone of the heart" to remind the listeners "that this is the risk we are running as a society – we are making a stone of too many hearts."

"It was imaginative and telling stuff, and makes one wonder what Charlie Haughey, Alan Dukes, Des O'Malley and Proinsias De Rossa will do when it's their turn," wrote journalist TP O'Mahony in *The Cork Examiner*.

Spring's leadership of the Labour Party had taken a dramatic turn upwards in Tralee. He had finally made the party more attractive to those who believe in a very moderate kind of socialism.

His new-found strength also allowed him to begin talks with The Workers' Party with a view to forging an alliance of the Left of some sort.

"For the time being Spring has the ball firmly in his hands," wrote John Horgan. "But as he contemplates the angle of his kick, however, he must be keenly conscious of the fact that, politically speaking, he is still uncomfortably close to his own goalposts, and that the opposing teams still control three-quarters of the field of play."

****

Back in Dáil Éireann Charles Haughey was again in the wars, most notably in a controversy over the beef industry.

Haughey had become closely aligned with Larry Goodman since he chaired a very high profile launch of a Goodman expansion plan in June 1987. But in March 1989 it was discovered that the Department of Agriculture had carried out a raid on a Goodman plant in north Dublin.

Barry Desmond was, in turn, accused by the Taoiseach of trying to sabotage the beef industry.

It was also disclosed that millions of pounds had been provided in export credit insurance for Goodman companies since Fianna Fáil had returned to office in 1987. The insurance was cancelled again in 1989 by Ray Burke when he was appointed Minister for Industry and Commerce.

In April 1989 Haughey returned home from a visit to Japan to find his Government teetering on the brink of defeat over a vote on a motion in Private Members' Time calling for an allocation of £400,000 to help haemophiliacs with AIDS. The Government lost by 72 votes to 69.

Haughey finally decided to go to the country on June 15, the same day as the European elections.

Labour and the other Opposition parties appeared to be much better prepared for an election than Fianna Fáil. They all pushed health issues to the fore while the relative good state of the economy was quietly forgotten. Fine Gael quickly joined with the PDs in a vote transfer arrangement deal, while Labour fought the campaign on their own with Spring firmly in control.

Labour continued to show a real rise in their level of support, as did The Workers' Party, and there was much talk of a real Left-Right divide in Irish politics.

In a pre-election interview in the *Irish Press* Dick Spring claimed that a "Right-Left axis" in Irish politics had emerged clearer than ever before.

"The Labour Party has led the fight back and people are beginning to realise there is very little to divide Fianna Fáil and Fine Gael – their ideological differences are minimal," he added.

Spring said he was more optimistic than ever about the long-term future for the Left in Ireland. "Even small farmers in Kerry are saying what we need now is more socialism because everything else has failed."

Spring claimed that Fianna Fáil, as a "catch-all" party, had finally come to an end. He admitted, however, that Labour did not have enough candidates of high calibre to take advantage of the upswing in the party's fortunes.

"Personally, I have more enthusiasm for the job than when I became party Leader. Rumours that I am leaving Kerry for Dublin or even the USA, are just that – rumour," he said.

He pledged the party to continue in Opposition, and not as part of any pact. But he admitted that Emmet Stagg was still viewed as a leader of the Left within the party: "Emmet is the Leader of the Left, there is a distinct group, they have their own meetings, they issue policy statements from time to time. I would be far happier if all that energy went into the mainstream of the party."

Well aware of his near defeat in the 1987 election, Spring concentrated much of his own personal efforts on his campaign in North Kerry and remained there for a good deal of the campaign.

While there he had to fight off a strong "red scare" campaign on him by the Taoiseach, Fine Gael and the PDs.

"The 'Red smear' campaign shows how desperate Fianna Fáil are to keep their support," he said in response. "In reality, the Labour Party is closer to Church thinking on social issues than any other party."

The turnout to voting at the general election in June was low and Fianna Fáil dropped four seats to 77. It was a bitter blow for Charles Haughey.

Fine Gael gained four seats, but not as many as they had anticipated, while the PDs were decimated, going down from 14 seats to six.

Labour and The Workers' Party gained support, but it was hardly the big breakthrough they had been hoping for. Labour was up four seats to 16, while The Workers' Party increased its representation from four to seven seats. Their percentage of the vote was back up to 9.5 per cent, from a low of 6.4 per cent in 1987.

The Greens also got their first TD elected.

Over in Fianna Fáil headquarters in Mount Street, Government Press Secretary PJ Mara was with Charles Haughey when the final results were announced.

"Seventy-seven and six makes eighty-three," said Mara. "Let's go for it!"

Down at the count in Tralee, matters were very different for Dick Spring. This time an effective campaign, combined with a sympathy vote, saw him re-elected on the first count with 10,118 first preference votes. He also managed to secure almost 30 per cent of the votes himself in number ones.

But Fine Gael, under the direction of Frank Quilter, was active again, this time with a "missing posters" campaign. Party organisers quietly removed a number of their own posters from prominent locations and then offered prize money for anyone who could find them. The "news item" generated considerable publicity at the time.

In the results of the European election there was good news for Labour, too. The wipe-out in the 1984 election was arrested when Barry Desmond took a seat in Dublin, polling over 57,000 votes, although a good deal less than The Workers' Party candidate, Proinsias De Rossa.

In Leinster, Michael Bell put up a brave fight until the eleventh count, but in Munster Eileen Desmond failed to capitalise on Labour's upsurge and polled poorly.

Back in Leinster House Dick Spring was off to a good start in the new Dáil when he challenged Charles Haughey on why he had not tendered his resignation when he was defeated in the first vote for Taoiseach on 29 June 1989. Haughey was forced to resign later in the day.

The move set a precedent whereby Spring was to take the limelight from Fine Gael as the new real Leader of the Opposition.

On 12 July Haughey was finally elected Taoiseach, with PD support, by 84 votes to 79.

On 4 September 1989, Dick Spring was involved in yet another car accident, although not serious.

The British Labour leader, Neil Kinnock, who had been on a weekend visit to Dublin, was on his way to Dublin airport when his chauffeur collapsed at the steering wheel. Beside him in the back of the car was his host over the three days, Dick Spring. Both had earlier watched a top-class Tipperary hurling team win the All-Ireland, after 17 years in the wilderness. The evening before Kinnock had familiarised himself with a camán when he accidentally met the Tipp hurlers outside the Burlington Hotel where they were staying.

Dublin chauffeur, Tom Conlon (52), had been driving the two leaders when he suffered a heart-attack.

The Mercedes limousine went out of control as it approached a roundabout at the airport end of the M1 motorway. It hit the car in front which in turn hit a lorry, which hit another car.

Spring, along with Neil Kinnock and his wife Glenys, emerged unscathed. Despite frantic efforts by Mr Kinnock and a retired nurse who happened to be passing to revive him, Mr Conlon died.

16

THE NEED FOR CHANGE

"These were the cute rural deputies, the 'culchies' of the Labour Party who could build a nest in your ear while minding mice at a crossroads."

These words, it has been argued, put Mary Robinson in Áras an Uachtaráin.

They were written by former Labour deputy Noel Browne, one of those considered as a possible candidate in the run-up to the November 1990 Presidential election.

The words were written about Dick Spring's father, Dan, for whose Dáil ability Browne had little regard. They offended Dick Spring's mother, Anna, who exerts considerable influence over her son.

"Now Mary Robinson, for instance, wouldn't have been her type of person," said one acquaintance. "She wouldn't have picked her as the Presidential candidate, but the problem was that the other candidate being considered was Noel Browne.

"There was a lot of affection for him in the party but he made the fatal mistake of passing some disparaging remarks about Dan Spring in his autobiography. Well ... that was the end of him, that one phrase could have been responsible for putting Mary Robinson in Áras an Uachtaráin."

Spring first put the idea of Labour running a candidate to his close friend, John Rogers, one Saturday evening in the Palace Bar in Dublin's Fleet Street in the early days of January 1990. The two often retired to the snug there for a few quiet pints after a day's work. The pub, a long-time watering hole for many distinguished writers and journalists, is a particular favourite of Rogers on his way from the Four Courts. He and the proprietor of the Palace, Liam Aherne, are good friends.

Today an etching of the Four Courts hangs in the snug of the Palace. The caption reads: "To John Rogers with many thanks. Mary Robinson. December 1990."

It was a "thank-you" present from the President to John Rogers to mark the historic discussion in the Palace. She subsequently presented all the members of her election committee with a similar print at a private celebratory dinner in the Áras.

Dick Spring favoured an election for the Presidency as there had been none since 1973, with the office being filled by agreement among the Dáil parties. If necessary, Spring declared, he would run himself to ensure that the people were given a choice.

Already Fianna Fáil, at the instigation of Charlie McCreevy and PJ Mara, had a very strong candidate in the shape of Brian Lenihan, who, although he had recently undergone major transplant surgery, was willing and ready to run.

"In addition, Dick Spring believed strongly that the Presidential election could be used as an opportunity to debate the future direction of the country, and to tap into the vote for change that he was convinced existed," wrote Fergus Finlay in his book *Mary Robinson – A President with a Purpose*.

It was Ruairí Quinn's personal assistant, Denise Rogers, who first mentioned the name of Mary Robinson as a candidate. Like other party workers, Denise panicked at the idea of Dick Spring running for office.

"At the time," she recalls, "Dick was working on a strategy for winning 25 Dáil seats. I felt his status as party Leader might be affected and he was needed to finish the job."

Various names were mentioned over coffee breaks in Leinster House, including Noel Browne, Justin Keating, and Conor Cruise-O'Brien. Barry Desmond's name came up, too.

Denise began to think seriously about who would be a good candidate.

"Suddenly the name of Mary Robinson dawned on me one morning as I was walking to work past the Mont Clare Hotel.

"She's someone who could really make a difference, if elected," she told her colleagues later that morning over coffee. Fergus Finlay took the suggestion back to Dick Spring.

But there were problems with Mary Robinson, not least that she was not even a member of the party, having resigned back in 1985.

Robinson had entered the Seanad in 1969 and, according to journalist Maire Crowe, writing in the *Irish Press* in 1985, had frequently "driven Parish Priests to pulpit fulminations" through the expression of her liberal opinions.

In November 1985 Robinson made what she described as "the hardest decision" of her life when she resigned from the Labour Party over the Anglo-Irish Agreement. Her reason – it could not be made acceptable to the Unionists.

"I'm only a modest cog in all of this, but I would rather fade out of politics totally than stay silent," she said.

Social legislation had always been to the fore in Robinson's political and legal life. The historic Airey case, family planning, divorce, opposition to the Special Criminal Court, advocacy of gay rights, had all been her concern. But the North of Ireland had also been an issue of real concern to her, and she maintained close contacts there.

Senator Robinson considered it a fundamental weakness of the Anglo-Irish Agreement that it had no support of any kind from among moderate Unionists. She resigned from the Labour Party.

"I find it surprising that people find it surprising that people would resign from a political party on principle; people don't do it much in this country," she said at the time.

She had expressed her disquiet at meetings of the New Ireland Forum along with Dáil deputies Frank Cluskey and Paddy Harte.

In an interview with *The Irish Times* prior to her resignation in May of 1985, she expressed doubts about Labour's commitment to equality and justice. She had a "break point", she admitted.

For all these reasons Robinson refused point blank to re-join the Labour Party in order to run for the Presidential election, and for a time the issue was a major stumbling block.

The decision on whether to run was an extremely difficult one for Robinson. A Robinson election worker recalls a story about Anne Lane, Mary Robinson's personal secretary. Back in the 1970s while practising as a barrister in Merrion Square she arrived into the office one day looking tired. When her secretary enquired was everything all right, Robinson replied that she was pregnant again.

"Oh, no!" declared Ann Lane. "More babies and bottles around the office!"

Now in the spring of 1990, back in her office at her home in Sandford Road, Ann Lane noticed the same tired look on Mary Robinson. Sleepless nights were all too obvious, although she said nothing for a few days.

Then came the familiar call.

"Ann, I've something to tell you," she said.

"Oh no!" declared Ann, "you're not pregnant again?"

"No," Robinson reassured her. "I'm going to run for the Presidency!"

Ann Lane was astonished, but not surprised. However, her immediate concern was a pre-booked climbing holiday in Kathmandu, later in the autumn when the election was due to be held. But there was a lot of time in between.

In making her decision to contest the election, Mary Robinson was strongly encouraged all the time to adopt an independent line by a close associate, Bride Rosney, then a school principal on the north side of Dublin.

Although not apparent at the time, Rosney was to exert a

major influence in the campaign in keeping a firm distance from both Labour and The Workers' Party. Throughout the campaign Rosney became a focus of tension with the Labour Party. She had formed the view that all the Labour Party hoped for, was to come in second, in front of Austin Currie, the Fine Gael candidate, while she saw heretofore untapped electoral votes available – and the ultimate prize of making it to the Áras.

In selecting Robinson, Spring had again defeated his old Left-wing foes Michael D Higgins and Emmet Stagg, who had both supported Noel Browne for the nomination.

Now Spring had secured the support of The Workers' Party and turned the campaign into a three-way fight with the Left, for once, united.

During the campaign Spring travelled occasionally with Robinson. Together they visited Irish emigrants in London. (Rosney claimed this was only because North Kerry TD Jimmy Deenihan had accompanied Austin Currie there on an earlier mission.)

In one interview in Ballyhaunis on local radio, Robinson bluntly said she was not putting forward Labour policies in the election when she was quizzed about what Labour had done for small farmers in the county.

"Well, damn it, she could have said we have eight rural TDs," muttered Dick Spring who was listening to the interview nearby.

The campaign continued, with often little more in common among the activists than the candidate herself.

Despite a controversial *Hot Press* interview in which Robinson had said she would perform the official opening of an illegal contraceptive stall in Dublin's Virgin Megastore, she was showing an impressive 32 per cent in the polls.

And then came the Lenihan tapes affair which resulted in the PDs threatening to pull out of Government if the Tánaiste remained in office.

In a Dáil confidence motion Dick Spring delivered a particularly stinging attack not just on Brian Lenihan and the tapes controversy, but on Charles Haughey.

"This debate is not about Brian Lenihan when it is all boiled down," he told the House. "This debate, essentially, is about an evil spirit that controls one political party in the Republic... This is a debate about greed for office, about disregard for truth, and about contempt for political standards. It is a debate about the way in which a once great party has been brought to its knees by the grasping acquisitiveness of its leader. It is ultimately about the cancer that is eating away at our body politic – and the virus which has caused that cancer, An Taoiseach, Charles J Haughey."

The speech was viewed as being particularly vicious, and caused offence to those both inside and outside Fianna Fáil.

In her book, *Candidate,* Emily O'Reilly pointed out that many found Spring's "cancer" metaphors particularly repellent as Haughey and Lenihan had both recently battled serious illness. Later that night, the Taoiseach sacked Brian Lenihan from his Cabinet, in one of the most traumatic happenings ever in Dáil Éireann.

The Robinson camp feared a huge sympathy vote would now go to Lenihan. Indeed, it appeared to be the case until the then Justice Minister, Pádraig Flynn, threw a spanner in the works in a controversial RTE radio interview.

Flynn accused Robinson of having "new interest in family, being a mother and all that kind of thing".

The Minister was immediately jumped on by the PDs' Michael McDowell who was also on the programme. The end result was an estimated loss of about 3 per cent to the Lenihan campaign, and victory for Mary Robinson.

It was an historic turnaround from any point of view and a sign of real change in Irish politics. It was the first time since the foundation of the State that the Presidency had been taken out of the hands of Fianna Fáil.

The significance was copperfastened by the size of the vote for Robinson in traditional rural areas. Overall, she won 39 per cent of the first preference vote. Her margin of victory in the second count was eight times bigger than that of Éamon de Valera in 1966.

In all, she won a majority in 25 of the 41 constituencies, although Lenihan won the first count in North Kerry, Dick Spring's base.

The results shook Irish politics to its roots. In Mary Robinson's own words, she had "rocked the system".

While the office of President is non-political, the election had the most profound effects on Irish politics. Within the Fine Gael Party, Leader Alan Dukes was gone in a matter of days, and John Bruton put in his place.

Fianna Fáil began a new exercise of soul-searching, with renewed emphasis on looking at its policies and becoming more open-minded on issues like divorce and homosexuality. Questions again began to be asked about Haughey's leadership.

But the biggest impact by far was for Labour, and Dick Spring.

The choice of Mary Robinson had proved absolutely correct, and Dick Spring could claim much of the credit. So, too, could Denise Rogers, who had the inspired idea outside the Mont Clare Hotel.

Spring's constant warnings that the people wanted change were proven true, and Labour was proved to be alive again and rid of the bad odour left after the ending of the Coalition Government in 1987.

His coup against the odds of putting Mary Robinson into the Phoenix Park, and beating the combined forces of Fianna Fáil and Fine Gael, crowned three years of achievement, and confirmed his role as the "real Leader of the Opposition" in the Dáil.

Spring quickly moved to capitalise on the victory by announcing a party shift to the Right, to social democracy.

The test now would be to turn the success into votes at the next general election. But there was still work to be done.

17

A POLITICAL LEGEND BOWS OUT

At 5.30pm on 25 July 1990, two closed envelopes lay in the bottom of a box at Labour Party headquarters in Dublin.

One envelope contained the name of Dick Spring, and the other Ruairí Quinn.

The time marked the close of nominations for the leadership and deputy leadership of the party as agreed at the last Annual Conference in Tralee.

It was decided there that the leadership election would be held in October 1990 by postal ballot of all party members.

Old foe Emmet Stagg had called for a postponement of the election so that it would not almost coincide with the Presidential election in November. Spring replied that as it was not possible to raise the issue of the leadership at a party conference for several years, the election could not be postponed. In the event, as there was only one nomination for each position, there was no election.

Spring described his single nomination as "a vote of confidence". Under party rules he was now the undisputed leader until 1996.

The aftermath of the Presidential election set a new goal for Dick Spring – to replace Fine Gael as the country's second largest political party. To this end Spring committed himself to a time frame of three general elections. But how exactly Labour would steal the ground from Fine Gael did not appear to have been thoroughly thought out.

In the run-up to the Annual Conference in April of 1991 there were plans to double the number of councillors in the June local elections of that year.

In general election terms, the strategy was to win a seat at the next election in every constituency where they had won a third of the quota in 1989. Constituencies specifically targeted were Dublin Central, Dublin North-West, Dún Laoghaire and Dublin South-Central.

Meanwhile, the party was banking on a gradual, slow decline in Government support as Albert Reynolds' budget was expected to come unstuck in its targets.

All the time Spring basked in the glow of the Presidential election result, which acted like money in the bank in terms of boosting his personal authority over the rank and file members.

Spring copperfastened his new grip on the party by bringing a new constitution before the Annual Conference in Killarney. He proposed to have it debated and passed without amendment.

Out went the old plough and stars logo, the aspiration to a 32-county socialist republic, the vow to nationalise the banks and other out-dated baggage of a bygone era.

In came a pretty red rose, a commitment to an open and mixed economy and lots more democracy. Commitment to equality was also stressed in the new constitution.

The constitution spelt out its recognition of the role of the private sector:

"...We want to build an economy in which there will be a role for both the private sector and for a dynamic, competitive public sector – an economy in which jobs will be created and protected for the benefit of all our people..."

Again the main thorn at the Killarney Conference, albeit a much less prickly one – was Emmet Stagg. Stagg broadly supported the document and agreed that the party needed modernising, but strongly believed that Spring's approach to the imposition of the new rules was anti-democratic.

In his address to the delegates Spring spelt out their new attitude to Coalition.

"...let there be no misunderstanding – the next time Labour goes into power, it will be on our own terms and nobody else's. The Labour Party does not exist to make up some other party's numbers, or as a convenience for any other party."

Welcoming the collapse of communism in Eastern Europe, Spring pointed out that the failure of the Eastern European model of socialism was not the end of the values that inspired Labour.

"The failed Communist models, to which some on the Left in Ireland have owed allegiance too long, failed to recognise the importance of basic individual freedom – that's why they collapsed," he said.

As expected, Spring referred again to Mary Robinson's victory as a sign of "the new and modern style of politics".

The Labour Leader made it clear that his immediate aim was to replace Fine Gael as the principal Opposition party.

At the conference, the motion to adopt the new constitution was carried by a majority of four to one. In the end the main arguments were about whether there had been enough consultation between the Leader and the grassroots, rather than on the contents.

Writing in the *Irish Press*, political correspondent Emily O'Reilly quoted one delegate who said the new constitution could sit equally well on the shoulders of Fine Gael or the PDs. Labour had come a long way.

"The constitution," said the delegate, "is sufficiently bland and non-specific to be broadly acceptable to most people." The remark was intended as an insult.

"What Spring and company have really done," wrote O'Reilly, " is to jettison the embarrassing bits (bank nationalisation and 32-county workers' republic stuff) and hang on to the bits that even raving fascists would find acceptable ... with the creeping deliberate 'blandification' of the party, future conferences may be reduced to the level of those held by the two bigger parties, where the only speech delegates bother to actually listen to is the Leader's address and the rest of the time is spent in beer and tittle-tattle."

O'Reilly's remarks were to be borne out at the Annual Conference in Waterford in 1993 when most of the delegates spent the day watching the Aintree Grand National "that never was", rather than listening to the babble in the small, stuffy conference room in Jury's Hotel.

But Spring left Killarney in 1991 with yet a firmer grasp than ever on the party. He had imposed his vision of future success and the means of achieving it.

His first electoral test soon arrived – the local elections in June.

At the last outing in 1985, Labour had felt the full wrath of the electorate and were reduced to 59 seats.

When the votes were counted, one of the surprising aspects was the low turnout, just 55.1 per cent of the electorate.

Labour didn't quite double its representation, but did manage an increase of 31 seats, bringing it up to a total of 90 nationwide. But its 10.6 per cent of the vote did not compare favourably with the 12.8 per cent won in 1974, or indeed the 14.8 per cent won in 1967. But it was a major boost, and an increase of more than 1 per cent on the general election figure of 1989.

The party achieved a particular victory in Limerick Corporation, where, due to the acquisition of Jim Kemmy in 1990, it became the largest party there. It also became the second largest party on Dublin Corporation.

In Tralee, Dick Spring, the only party Leader to run in the elections, raised many eyebrows when, in the true family tradition, he chose to run without a team mate.

He topped the poll with almost 3,000 first preferences. A surplus of 1,200 votes was entirely wasted. (Fianna Fáil, which won only 1.4 quotas, secured two seats).

His sister, Maeve, did, however, win a seat in mid-Kerry.

So it was a happy Dick Spring who relaxed in Dublin's Burlington Hotel on Saturday, 26 October 1991 at a dinner to mark his ten years as Leader of the Party.

British Labour Leader, Neil Kinnock, was among the 500 guests who forked out £100 a plate to help pay off the debts of the Mary Robinson campaign.

An old friend from the rugby world, BBC broadcaster Cliff Morgan, was a second guest speaker. A "This Is Your Life" video was also shown and among those who appeared on screen to pay tribute to Spring were Brian Lenihan and Garret FitzGerald.

****

Meanwhile, back in Leinster House the roof was continuing to fall in on Charles Haughey.

In August 1990, the Dáil had been re-convened especially to save the Goodman organisation from total collapse.

Spring made a well-researched contribution to the debate. It is arguable that his speech on that day spelt the death-knell for Alan Dukes' leadership of Fine Gael as it was later revealed that bankers had come to the socialist Dick Spring with inside information, fearing that Fine Gael would not use it effectively.

In May of 1991, ITV broadcast what was claimed to be an exposé of operations at Larry Goodman meat plants, leading to a full one-day Dáil debate on the affair. It eventually led to the setting up of the Beef Tribunal.

In September the Greencore controversy erupted.

The story, by journalist Sam Smyth, told of how the Chief Executive of the Irish Sugar Company, Chris Comerford, was suing the directors of a Jersey-based company, Talmino, which had sold its stake in a subsidiary of the Sugar Company, Irish Sugar Distributors. Comerford claimed he owned a stake in Talmino.

The implications for the Government were serious as the Minister for Agriculture, Michael O'Kennedy, had direct responsibility to oversee the company. Comerford resigned.

Spring was to the fore in the Dáil in bringing accusations against the Government. In parliamentary terms, he was having a field day.

As the Greencore controversy intensified, Government Press Secretary, PJ Mara, accused Spring of being the mouth-piece of Chris Comerford.

A series of intense exchanges between Haughey and Spring followed.

Throughout September and October 1991, Spring issued a series of statements criticising the Government in its handling of the affair.

In early November Haughey hit back. He claimed that Spring had made representations to the late Ruadhri Roberts to secure the appointment of Chris Comerford to the post of Chief Executive of the Sugar Company. Spring rejected the claim in a detailed statement to the media. The battle continued.

The Goodman and Greencore sagas were further complicated by yet more scandals, including one involving the purchase of a new headquarters in Ballsbridge by Telecom Éireann.

During a subsequent briefing with political correspondents, PJ Mara posed the question about Spring's association with Pat Doherty, a property developer involved in the Telecom controversy. However, Doherty confirmed in an interview that he "had no association of any kind" with Spring. He had met him once, many years before, at a function in London.

"The whole thing is laughable," Doherty added. "I don't understand what they are looking for. There is nothing there."

There were further controversies surrounding Celtic Helicopters, owned by the Taoiseach's son Ciaran, and surrounding the sale of Carysfort College to UCD by Pino Harris, a Fianna Fáil supporter.

In the Carysfort controversy Spring claimed that Haughey had "forfeited the right to office", because of his alleged personal involvement in the sale.

Eventually a vote of No Confidence in Haughey caused two Ministers, Albert Reynolds and Pádraig Flynn to be sacked.

When Donegal TD, Dr Jim McDaid, was appointed Minister for Defence, The Workers' Party Leader, Proinsias De Rossa, caused uproar when he pointed out that McDaid had been involved in an extradition case in 1990 involving IRA man, James Pius Clarke. McDaid withdrew his name in the Dáil. He had been Minister for Defence for eight hours.

The sordid affair, started by Proinsias De Rossa, was then taken up by Fine Gael. Strangely, Dick Spring, who had been spearheading the attack on the Taoiseach, kept his distance.

In a Dáil speech on 14 November, Spring said that statements that Jim McDaid was a "fellow traveller" of the IRA were unworthy of the people who made them.

"...the explicit accusations that were levelled against him were not based on any detailed examination of his track record. He was, in effect, tried, condemned and executed on the basis of one incident...I wonder how many Members of this House could withstand that sort of campaign if it were based on one incident in the past on any of us?"

Mr Spring went on say he hoped Deputy McDaid would recover from the events, and that Charles Haughey should resign over his incompetence in the affair.

Then the telephone tapping controversy of 1982 re-emerged when former Justice Minister Seán Doherty claimed the Taoiseach had known that the telephones of two journalists were tapped.

Spring was relentless in his attacks on Haughey, whom he described as a man who lusted after office and who believed that "with enough brass neck he could deflect any legitimate suspicion away from himself and onto others".

"All of these scandals have one thing in common," he said. "They all derive from a style of Government that is contemptuous of any demand that it accounts for itself, and is unable to even comprehend the need for standards. The origins of that style of Government must be traced, without any apology, to the lust for office of one man..."

Spring concluded by making a now familiar demand – the resignation of one, Charles Haughey.

Finally on 22 January when the PDs threatened to leave government, Haughey decided to resign rather than cause a general election.

In the Dáil on 11 February Spring was fulsome in his praise of the retiring Taoiseach. In his speech he referred to Haughey's quotation the previous week from Shakespeare's *Julius Caesar* – "The Heavens themselves blaze forth the death of princes."

Mark Antony, in the same play, had said: "I come to bury Caesar, not to praise him."

However, Spring said he would resist the temptation to follow Mark Antony's precedent and instead, would turn to Flann O'Brien to pay tribute to a retiring political legend.

In his tribute to another folk-hero, Finn McCool, O'Brien said:

"I am an Ulsterman, a Connachtman and a Greek,

I am my own father and my son,

I am every hero from the crack of time."

It was the end, said Spring, of a long, turbulent era in Irish politics. Haughey had been elected Leader of Fianna Fáil and Taoiseach in an atmosphere of high expectation.

He had brought a prodigious range of talents and skills to the job, unparalleled in the modern era, with an ambition and hunger for office with which his name would always be associated.

On a personal level, Dick Spring said he had always found Charles Haughey courteous and fair, and he hoped his talents would find a true expression, perhaps in the further development of the cultural life of the country, to which he had a genuine and long-standing commitment.

18

CHANGE

The day Albert Reynolds took over as Taoiseach, there was an anxious message from the Attorney General, Harry Whelehan, to meet him.

Mr Whelehan had referred a threat by a young pregnant girl to the High Court, who claimed she had been raped, to go to England to seek an abortion. She was doing so with the co-operation of her parents.

The High Court subsequently ruled that she could not leave the country with the wilful intention of seeking an abortion. The ruling caused a major controversy, known as the "X" case, which was ultimately to lead to a referendum later in 1992.

Giving his reaction on 19 February, Dick Spring claimed the judgment represented new law which involved the most frightening consequences. Effectively, the High Court had decided that it was appropriate that a citizen from Ireland could be prevented from travelling to another country for purposes that were entirely legal in that jurisdiction.

Further, the court had decided that the State now had the right to intervene in a situation which, in every other country in the western world, would be considered an entirely private, family matter.

Spring also argued that the injunction now appeared to be available to any person wishing to prevent an abortion, including an evil and depraved man who wished to force his victim to carry a child conceived through violence.

Spring criticised the Attorney General for not establishing

the condition of the mother before referring it to the courts. He called for the situation to be urgently reviewed by the Law Reform Commission.

The High Court decision was appealed to the Supreme Court which, in an unexpected judgment, ruled that abortion was lawful in the State under certain limited circumstances where suicidal tendencies could be proved.

In April, the Government decided to hold a referendum on the right to travel and information when the EC refused permission for an amendment, which dealt with the right to life, to be inserted into the Maastricht Protocol. The decision was welcomed by Dick Spring, who, however, argued that the referendum be held in advance of the Maastricht referendum, scheduled for June.

In early May, Spring called on the Irish people to vote "Yes" to the Maastricht Treaty despite the fact that the protocol had caused a "dilemma of conscience" for many. (Michael D Higgins and Emmet Stagg indicated that they would be voting "No".)

Despite the fact that Labour had opposed Ireland's entry to the EEC in 1973, Dick Spring now threw his weight behind the Maastricht campaign, as pretending otherwise was, he claimed, "foolish, dangerous and dishonest".

Another contentious issue, the European Common Defence Policy, would have to be faced in 1996.

"We must be ready," he said. "We could influence the debate about militarism if we worked hand in hand with the other neutral countries which had applied to join the EC."

Some members of the Community harboured ambitions to turn the European Union into the European pillar of NATO, but a bloc of four, he claimed, and possibly five, if Switzerland was included, would have their own strong views on Cold War military alliances.

"Our task will be to work with the other neutrals to develop policies for peaceful security," he said.

He deplored statements by Fine Gael and Fianna Fáil which implied that neutrality was a thing of the past.

Emphasising that this decision was not to be taken in the 18 June referendum, he added: "Whenever that question is put to the people, I will urge them to adhere to a foreign policy based on the principle of peace, not militarism."

On the abortion issue, he said the protocol to the Maastricht Treaty to protect Article 40.3.3 of the Constitution was inserted in secrecy to appease a small and voluble section of Irish opinion, but it had exploded in the face of the Government.

Regarding the creation of a common currency, Mr Spring said Ireland would benefit more from joining than remaining outside. But the conditions of entry to the final stage would have to be framed so that they did not add to the country's unemployment problem.

On the EC Social Charter dealing with the rights of workers – and from which Britain had been granted exemption – he said its implementation was a battle to be fought.

Spring's attitude drew criticism from some Labour quarters. One of those who quit the party was Donncha O hEalaithe, a lecturer at Galway Regional Technical College, who accused Spring of an *"uno duce, una voce"* attitude to Maastricht.

On 9 June, nine days before the referendum, Spring joined the Taoiseach, Albert Reynolds, John Bruton and Des O'Malley outside Leinster House in calling for a "Yes" vote. The move left those opposing the Treaty in the Dáil to members of Democratic Left and the sole Workers' Party and Green Party deputies.

The four Leaders committed themselves in a six-page document to the holding of a referendum in the autumn on the right to travel and information and to bringing proposals for constitutional changes arising in the "X" case before the Dáil as soon as was practicable.

However, despite the apparent agreement between the Leaders, there was disagreement over the status of the Maastricht Treaty in the event of Denmark refusing to ratify it (it did subsequently). Mr Reynolds insisted it remained valid until one or more countries refused to lodge the instruments of ratification.

The unanimity of the political Leaders on the basic question of acceptance of the Maastricht Treaty ensured that it was carried by a huge majority on voting day, 18 June.

In the run-up to the autumn referendum on the right to travel and information, the Government added a third proposal on the issue of abortion. All three wordings were drafted by a Cabinet sub-committee which included the Leader of the Progressive Democrats, Des O'Malley.

There was little difficulty with the wordings on the right to travel and information, but the third part of the referendum, which outlawed the termination of pregnancy, unless it was necessary to save the life, as distinct from the health of the mother, caused grave disquiet.

Spring described it as "brutal and divisive", and would ultimately be a counter-attack on the basic rights of Irish citizens.

"It is simply not acceptable to us, and it never will be, that our Constitution should set out to treat half our citizens differently, just because those citizens are women," he declared.

"We are going to put into our Constitution, if this Government has its way," he continued, "a provision that will require doctors, and nobody else, to determine what might be a Constitutional abortion and what might not. That is more than an absurdity. It is an obscenity."

In the November referendum the electorate voted strongly in favour of inserting the provisions on the right to travel and the right to information, but overwhelmingly rejected the wording on the right to life.

The right to travel amendment was carried by 62.3 per cent for, with 37.7 per cent against, the right to information by 59.9 per cent for, with 40.1 per cent against, and the abortion wording was rejected by 65.4 per cent to 34.6 per cent.

In Dick Spring's home constituency the figures were much closer, with the wording on the right to information carried by a bare 0.5 per cent.

In the event of a rejection, the Taoiseach, Mr Reynolds, had already promised to introduce legislation to accommodate the court ruling in the "X" case.

During the campaign, the Minister for Health, Dr John O'Connell, had published legislation proposing that a special number of consultants in approved hospitals would be empowered to direct that abortion should take place if a real and substantial risk to the life of the mother existed.

The Labour Party proposed that any new abortion legislation should be referred to the Supreme Court for a test of its constitutionality.

****

The spring of 1992 also saw a number of other developments on the political front.

In February The Workers' Party finally split when party Leader Proinsias De Rossa narrowly failed to reform the party and broaden its democracy.

Six deputies left to form an interim party, first named New Agenda, and later Democratic Left. The move left The Workers' Party decimated with just one Dáil deputy, Tomás Mac Giolla.

As the new party emerged, Labour Leader Dick Spring

questioned the need for competing political organisations on the Left. But he recognised that for the time being, a number of deputies would "remain committed to the idea of a separate organisation", with an "economic and social division not dissimilar to ours".

At the end of March, Spring launched the "Labour 2000 Campaign," a move aimed at ensuring "that Labour had the dominant message in Irish politics by the end of this decade". Again he repeated the goal of becoming the second largest party in the Dáil "in the short to medium term".

Launching the campaign, he emphasised the theme that was to dominate the party for the remainder of the year, "Change".

"There is a new movement in Ireland, a new spirit for change. It's about finding new answers to major economic issues. It's about openness, new and higher standards of public life, participation... In fact it's about extending the concept of citizenship to include forgotten and neglected groups as equal partners in our community."

Spring also re-shuffled his Front Bench and announced the names of spokespersons who were not Members of the Dáil, but "who will be after the next election". They included Senator Pat Upton, Senator John Ryan, Senator Joe Costello, and Councillors Niamh Bhreathnach, Eithne Fitzgerald, Brian Fitzgerald, Derek McDowell and Seán Kenny.

The end of March saw Spring in London at the invitation of the British Labour spokesman on Northern Ireland, Kevin McNamara, to help canvass the Irish vote during the election there. Spring concentrated his efforts on seats in Tooting and Hornsey, where the Irish vote can add significantly to the outcome.

In September, the Beef Tribunal was again back in the headlines when the issue of Cabinet confidentiality was raised during the hearing of evidence from former Justice Minister Ray Burke.

The issue, which was subsequently referred to the High Court and Supreme Court, meant that the Tribunal could never hear details on the discussions surrounding the crucial issue of export credit insurance, and how much of it was to be granted to Larry Goodman.

Spring reacted by publishing the text of a Bill to change the Constitution to waive confidentiality, if it was considered necessary. The Bill was aimed at protecting the principle of confidentiality, but would also enable the High Court and Supreme Court to allow disclosure of Cabinet proceedings if such disclosure was considered to be in the public interest.

"The Taoiseach is absolutely and fundamentally wrong to dismiss any idea of changing the law," he said. "The blanket provision of executive privilege, which has been instituted by the Supreme Court interpretation of the Constitution as it stands, reveals a dangerous gap in our Constitutional provisions.

"A situation where the motivation of decisions made in the Cabinet room can never be questioned, or investigated, is impractical, unworkable and inherently dangerous. It cannot be allowed to go unchallenged."

In October the Taoiseach took the stand at the Tribunal and, giving evidence, accused his Industry Minister, Des O'Malley, of being "dishonest" concerning the amount of money owed to the Exchequer under the terms of the export credit insurance scheme.

Despite a number of opportunities, Mr Reynolds refused to withdraw the serious accusation.

O'Malley reacted promptly and made it clear that unless the charges were withdrawn, his party would leave Government. Reynolds refused to budge and on 6 November, Des O'Malley, Bobby Molloy and Mary Harney submitted their resignations.

O'Malley's press conference in the Mont Clare Hotel revealed that relations between Fianna Fáil and the PDs had been extremely poor since Reynolds had taken over from Charles Haughey.

Among other things, O'Malley revealed that he had written to the Taoiseach in September of 1992 to protest at the departure from Cabinet procedures through an emerging pattern of non-consultation. The revelation showed that the Cabinet had barely been hanging together during its last months of existence.

In his speech on the motion of No Confidence which brought down the Government on 5 November, Dick Spring was again scathing of the Fianna Fáil Government. He singled out Albert Reynolds for particular attack:

"This is the Taoiseach who preaches about respect for the institutions of this House, but who has lost the ability to conduct himself with dignity in any crisis.

"This is a Taoiseach who promised open Government, but whose Government fought in the Supreme Court to establish a system of Cabinet secrecy that flies in the face of that promise.

"This is the Taoiseach who talks about consensus, but who governs behind closed doors....

"The politics of stunts, strokes and scandals must be brought to an end once and for all. We represent a mature and sophisticated people – it is time that we gave them the democracy they deserve."

19

A ROTATING TAOISEACH

Dick Spring was quick off the mark to tell the electorate that the Labour Party would offer the country "a new deal" in its election manifesto. The election, he said, would be about two issues: putting trust back into politics, and justice back into economics.

He announced that the party would be running 40 candidates in 34 of the 41 constituencies with MEP Barry Desmond as Director of Elections.

From the beginning he refused to be drawn on the question of a possible Coalition with Fianna Fáil, or other parties, merely repeating that his aim was to maximise the number of Labour seats.

Labour would concentrate on the crisis in housing and in the health services, and "could not contemplate entering into a relationship with any other parties unless they tackled serious problems like this".

Labour, he claimed, would not be involved "in mud-slinging or in personality attacks during the campaign".

The party would play a strong and vigorous role in the new Dáil "whatever the outcome".

Spring launched his party's manifesto at two high-powered press conferences in Dublin's Riverside Centre on Sir John Rogerson's Quay on 11 and 18 November.

Among the proposals put forward were ideas for a National Economic and Social Forum (NESF) which would have a very wide representation and have an independent chairperson, the establishment of a third banking force based on a combination of the ACC, the ICC, the Trustee Savings Banks and An Post, possibly in a joint venture with a major European bank.

Spring pointed out that there was a huge and unrealised potential for additional sources of savings and investments. Such a financial organisation would bring about much needed competition in the banking sector.

The proposals included plans for a new Department of Enterprise and Employment, as well as a new Department of Trade. There were proposals, too, for increasing the number of local authority houses and the number of gardaí.

He spoke of accelerating such projects as the Tallaght Regional Hospital, light rail for Dublin, national sports facilities, county roads and tourism projects.

To pay for the extra spending, Labour proposed to increase public borrowing by £360 million as a "short term measure".

The party was not hostile to the private sector, but public enterprise would be efficient and dynamic. In particular Aer Lingus and Bord na Móna would be provided with further State equity.

The second document, published on 18 November, dealt in detail with children and people with a disability. Spring promised a full Cabinet Minister for the handicapped:

"It will be a fundamental priority for Labour that any new Government elected in Ireland should designate a Minister with special and overall responsibility for the rights of people with a disability," said the document. "That Minister must be a full member of the Cabinet, and must be given a budget which is commensurate to the task."

Legislation would be enacted to establish the rights of people with a mental handicap on a statutory basis, together with a means of redress for people whose rights were ignored.

He also promised a detailed examination of a scheme to provide an allowance for people with a disability to employ a personal assistant where they required help at home.

The document proposed a major plan of Oireachtas reform, with MEPs to be given a role in Oireachtas committees, and the compulsory disclosure by political parties and candidates of all financial contributions.

There would be a repeal of all British legislation enacted before Independence. A constituency commission would be set up, on a statutory basis with its remit extending to local electoral areas and European constituencies. Local government reform would include the establishment of regional authorities and sub-county structures, to be elected in July 1993.

In the area of social welfare, Spring promised to reverse cuts made by the outgoing Minister, Charlie McCreevy, the so-called "Dirty Dozen", within twelve months.

On education, the party said it would extensively re-draft the Government's Green Paper to reflect real priorities, and work towards a position where the income limit for higher education grants was based on net income, rather than gross income.

On the morning of 11 November in an interview with RTE's Michael Ryan at Waterford Airport, Spring dropped a bombshell. He said he wanted to be a rotating Taoiseach in any Coalition with another political party.

The news hit the headlines instantly, and stole much of the thunder from the Fianna Fáil manifesto which was launched later that afternoon.

The Irish Times political reporter, Deaglán de Bréadún, was accompanying the Labour Leader. Assessing the idea of a rotating Taoiseach, he wrote: "Albert Reynolds could go to the races more often and Dick Spring would have more time to read novels or listen to Bob Dylan."

The Labour Party supporters loved it as they greeted their Leader's campaign bus in places like Carrick-on-Suir, Clonmel,

Kilkenny and Wexford.

In Carlow a presenter at the local radio station, Christy Walsh, leaned from the window as Dick Spring was approaching.

"Good evening, Taoiseach!" he shouted.

"If Bill Clinton can do it, I don't see why I can't," replied Spring.

The Labour Leader pointed out that in Finland and Italy a prime minister's appointment was not conditional on having obtained a majority. In Israel the job alternated between two politicians.

Spring's message echoed one of the songs of his hero, Bob Dylan – "The Times They are a-Changing".

Again and again he shouted out the message: "It's time for change in Irish politics, and the Labour Party will lead that change."

The campaign song blaring out of the campaign bus was by a Dylan disciple, Tom Petty, who sang: "I won't back down".

As the Labour Leader was walking through Carrick-on-Suir his attention was drawn to the building where Daniel O'Connell opened the first office of the National Bank on 28 January 1835. The treasurer of the Labour branch in the town, Ed Holloway, wanted to take a picture of Spring in front of the plaque commemorating O'Connell.

"There was a Kerryman here before me," quipped Spring.

A passer-by saw another humorous side.

"Is this a hold-up?" he asked.

It was freely acknowledged by Labour supporters, including off-the-record briefing from Fergus Finlay, that the idea of Dick Spring for Taoiseach was thrown out as a measure of the high price which he would exact from any future Coalition partner.

Spring made it clear that he was fed up with other parties, notably Fine Gael, who appeared to assume that he would be readily available as a dancing partner in a "rainbow" Coalition that included the PDs.

"Fine Gael could not roll into the dance hall late at night, half cut, and assume that Little Miss Labour would still be waiting demurely for them to take her out on the floor," wrote Deaglán de Bréadún.

"Nor," he continued, "should they take it for granted that when the music stopped the same Miss Labour would consent to a long-term liaison or even to 'come outside for a minute' just because, in a moment of impetuous generosity, Mister Fianna Fáil or Fine Gael bought her a bottle of lemonade."

As things stood, the FF or FG request for a dance could be met with the legendary and much quoted response which might even have been first uttered in one of Albert Reynolds' dance halls: "Ask me sister, I'm sweatin'!"

Asked to comment on Spring's claims to share in the leadership of a future Coalition, the Taoiseach, Albert Reynolds, said dismissively: "It is an interesting aspiration of Mr Spring's. I leave it to himself to work it out." On the other hand, PD Leader Des O'Malley was quick to point out that the idea "would not be impossible".

On the same day as Spring was in the south-east of the country, Reynolds announced a £750 million jobs fund as part of his party's manifesto.

The Labour Leader described it as the "back-door privatisation of the ACC, the ICC and the remaining State shareholdings in Irish Life and Greencore".

Already Spring was predicting that his party would come back with "more than 20 Dáil seats".

On the morning of 12 November, Spring was back in Dublin's Shelbourne Hotel presenting the party's women candidates to the press. Their ambition was to shatter the "glass ceiling" for women in politics, a ceiling which still acted as a barrier to their advancement.

It was a good morning for Labour. The opinion polls were showing them at a historically high 17 per cent.

Then he headed for Drogheda and Mullingar, rural towns where a junior ministry is known as the "half car". Spring was now making it clear that he was looking for the "half jet".

"The canonisation of Dick Spring, the Leader of the Labour Party, is the pivotal phenomenon in this general election," wrote Geraldine Kennedy, then public affairs correspondent of *The Irish Times*. "He is admired left, right and centre in the opinion polls."

Spring had now reached such Olympian heights that it was forgotten that Peter Barry had once described him as "a sheep in sheep's clothing".

This time, as in 1989, Spring was also keeping an eye on the home constituency of North Kerry.

It was an intense battle again there for two seats between Fianna Fáil's Tom McEllistrim against Dick Spring and Fine Gael's Jimmy Deenihan. This time Fianna Fáil was the party under most pressure with outgoing TD McEllistrim likely to be fighting for his survival with his FF running mate Denis Foley.

The competition flared up outside churches as the parties vied to be first to address the Mass-goers. Outside Ballyheigue church gate, the war erupted.

"We've been out since early morning," said the Fianna Fáil man.

"What do you think I've been doing," retorted Spring, "sitting on my backside?"

Such were the joys of canvassing on the second Sunday of the campaign, even though you might be the most popular politician in the country.

A few miles further on the perplexed flock emerging from 10am Mass at Kilmoyley negotiated their way through TV cameras, notebooks and strangers. Spring grabbed as many hands as he could before heading on to Ardfert.

Right across the constituency Dick Spring's Volvo Estate car, with a special back support for Spring in the passenger's seat, was desperately seeking out church gates.

The mood was summed up by a bar owner in Tralee:

"When the business community thinks about a new factory for Tralee, they're going to put in someone who they believe can provide it. Tom McEllistrim had his chance and did nothing. Now, let's see what Spring can do."

In Kerry, Kristi Spring was again fully involved in the campaign. In an *The Irish Times* interview she remarked that she had "developed a respectful enthusiasm for elections". On the door steps people were asking him about her. "She's had an extraordinary impact," he added.

"The primary thing for both of us is making sure that the kids aren't disrupted in any way. Kristi's mother has flown in from America to look after that end, so it's all hands to the pump from the American end of the family."

In Dublin, Labour canvassers were having unexpected experiences. In the Dublin Central constituency two of them were surprised to be offered drugs for sale while they dropped leaflets into flats.

"D'ya want gear?" they were asked.

"No. Votes."

"If you took some gear you'd get around quicker."

"If we took some gear we might wake up in the PDs!"

"Yeah. Bad scene, that."

On the morning of 20 November Spring had breakfast with *The Irish Times* journalist Tom Humphries.

Spring was angry over a front page piece about him.

"Never mind that," said tour manager Pat Magner. "I'll put a bit of jizz into him. He's always better that way."

Spring returned from a radio interview, jizzed up.

"It's remarkable," he began, "the adrenalin levels are so high. I wake up at six every morning even if I don't have to be up until seven. It might be four o'clock in the afternoon before I think of breakfast, and then it's just coffee.

"At nine o'clock in the evening I have to grab something that makes up for the three meals I have missed. The one thing I really hate about canvassing is when it rains. I don't like being wet. It has rained only once so far. How can I complain?"

But he was already dismissive of the idea of a rainbow Coalition:

"I do know we were flying out of Knock on Tuesday and the press spotted a rainbow and were very excited. But before the cameras could catch the thing, it just happened to fade away. That's what rainbows do.

"The bottom line is simple," he continued. "The Labour Party isn't available on the basis of propping up another party. We are in the business of changing the face of Irish politics. They said it couldn't be done. They were right about Guinness Light. They were wrong about Mary Robinson. They are wrong about the Labour Party. Whoever 'they' are."

But neither were relations at all smooth with Fianna Fáil. Worried by the alarming show of support for Labour, Fianna Fáil – backed up by a team of Saatchi & Saatchi advisers – launched a scathing attack on Labour's policies.

On 22 November, a few days before polling day, Brian Cowen claimed that Labour's real policies were contained in a document "Labour's Agenda" adopted at the 1989 Annual Conference. It contained proposals for a 3 per cent residential property tax on houses valued in excess of £50,000, a farm tax, the PRSI ceiling to be abolished, as well as the abolition of mortgage interest and VHI tax reliefs.

Spring retaliated by saying he was very angry at the type of advert "imported by Fianna Fáil from Saatchi & Saatchi across the water," and that the advertisements were a personalised, misleading dirty-tricks campaign.

In an interview on RTE's *This Week* programme on 22 November, Spring said his own preference was for Fianna Fáil and Fine Gael to get together in Government. But whatever decision Labour made, it would be taken at a special delegate conference. He said a Coalition with Fianna Fáil was "practicably unworkable".

In an interview with this writer in the *Irish Press* he spoke of the enormous problems there would be with a "discredited Taoiseach".

He dismissed Fianna Fáil's proposals for a "warehouse"company with a £750 million jobs fund as a "nonsense". He would have no part in any such concoction.

"Fianna Fáil did not even treat the PDs with the status of a mudguard, but with about the status of a screw on the rear wheel, almost unnecessary, and only needed on a bad bend," he added.

Questioned on the idea of a rotating Taoiseach, he said the response he had been getting at the doors suggested he should "forget about the rotating part". People were telling him he should be full Taoiseach. He cited the Italian Leader, Bettino Craxi, who had been appointed Prime Minister with only 8 per cent of the vote.

On the eve of the election there was good news from the Left for Spring when Democratic Left leader, Proinsias De Rossa, confirmed that his party would support the candidacy of Dick Spring for Taoiseach in the new Dáil.

In their television debate, both Albert Reynolds and John Bruton claimed they would both be in a position to form a Government after the election.

In a typical comment, Albert Reynolds said he would be "there or thereabouts" when it came to forming a new Government.

Spring asked supporters to give their transfers to those parties of the Left whose policies were closest to Labour's.

Meanwhile, PD Leader Des O'Malley predicted that his party would form a key element in any new Government.

The scene was set for the formation of the 27th Dáil.

20
SUPERMAN SPRING

For Fianna Fáil and Fine Gael the outcome of the general election of 25 November 1992, was a disaster. But the Labour Party had produced its best ever result.

Fianna Fáil, with 68 seats, had lost nine and received its lowest percentage of first preference votes since 1927 when it first entered the Dáil.

Fine Gael lost ten seats, and was now at its lowest level since 1948 in its percentage of first preference votes (45 seats).

The Progressive Democrats also suffered a reduction in their first preference vote, but increased their number of Dáil seats from six to ten.

Democratic Left were reduced to four seats and The Workers' Party lost their one sitting deputy. The Greens held their one outgoing seat, but with a change of deputy.

In contrast, Labour had received its best vote ever with 19.3 per cent of the first preference votes, an increase of almost 10 per cent on the 1989 figure. The most significant factor was the rate at which their support soared upwards during the course of the campaign – and also a worrying factor that this could be a very transitory happening.

In an MRBI poll on 30 September, eight weeks before the election, Labour registered only 12 per cent in the polls. In the final MRBI poll on 20 November it had shot up to 22 per cent. A Lansdowne opinion poll, published in the *Sunday Press* on 22 November showed exactly the same figure.

"Thus, over a third of Labour's vote may be a volatile one, which may abandon the party as quickly as it embraced it," wrote Vincent Browne in the *Sunday Tribune*.

With 33 seats Dick Spring had finally made the breakthrough he had always dreamed of for his party. Twice previously it had reached a peak of 22 seats – once in 1927 when it won 12.6 per cent of the vote and again in 1965 with 15.4 per cent of the vote. However, the party recorded its highest ever first preference vote of 17 per cent in 1969 when it won only 18 seats.

The Party had made spectacular gains in Dublin with a deputy elected in nine of the eleven constituencies, and two in Dublin North-East and Dublin South-West. The party also topped the poll in nine Dublin constituencies.

Such was the extent of their victory – epitomised by poll-topper Eithne Fitzgerald in Dublin South – that they could have secured at least two more seats in the capital had they run second candidates.

The party also made history with the election of Dr Mossajee Bhamjee, a psychiatrist originally from South Africa, in Clare.

All out-going deputies, except Michael Moynihan in South Kerry, who had retired, were returned along with newcomers John Mulvihill (Cork East), Joe Costello (Dublin Central), Seán Kenny (Dublin North-East), Derek McDowell (Dublin North-Central), Roísín Shorthall (Dublin North-West), Eithne Fitzgerald (Dublin South), Pat Upton (Dublin South-Central), Eamon Walsh (Dublin South-West), Niamh Bhreathnach (Dún Laoghaire), John Ryan Tipperary North), Willie Penrose (Westmeath), Declan Bree (Sligo-Leitrim), Tommy Broughan (Dublin North-East), Mossajee Bhamjee (Clare), Breda Moynihan-Cronin (Kerry South), Joan Burton (Dublin West), Pat Gallagher (Laois-Offaly) and Brian Fitzgerald (Meath).

Down in his home constituency Superman Spring soared over everyone else in the election with 11,515 first preference votes, or 34 per cent of the total.

This was mainly at Fianna Fáil's expense, but as they were never expected to win more than one seat, it made little difference except in the replacement of long-standing deputy Tom McEllistrim by Denis Foley.

The contrast between McEllistrim's defeat and Spring's victory was particularly poignant. Between his father and himself the McEllistrim family had given 69 years service to the people of North Kerry, much more than the Spring family.

But as Tom McEllistrim was speaking at the end of the count, Dick Spring was already on a plane on his way to Dublin for talks. He was reigning spectacularly, McEllistrim sadly retreating.

Earlier in the day, Spring broke with family tradition by arriving at the count at the Earl of Desmond Hotel at lunchtime. Already it was evident that North Kerry had swung to Labour.

He walked into the count centre with all the confidence of a Kerry football captain bringing home the Sam Maguire Cup.

His first comment, as he watched the RTE monitor, was that a red tide was "wiping away the older order". But for most of the day he locked himself away in room 65 of the hotel which had suddenly become the pivot of political power in the Republic.

In a live television link at 4pm, he was congratulated by Dublin Lord Mayor Gay Mitchell, who said the first Government was formed in the Mansion House and his door was always open to Spring. With typical wry humour Spring replied that he already had accommodation in Dublin.

Asked how he would feel about going into Coalition with Fianna Fáil, Spring replied: "I sure would not feel great about it." He added that he was "saddened more than hurt" by Fianna Fáil attacks on him and said he greatly favoured legislation which would cap the amount of money being spent on election campaigns.

For the first time he also hinted that he might consult with groups outside the Dáil about the type of country they wanted. But it was already evident in the Earl of Desmond Hotel that Labour had lost out by not fielding enough candidates.

"And there was knowledge, too," wrote one commentator, "that Spring could fumble another ball and, if he does not make the correct decisions, cause another election."

With most of the votes in on the night of 26 November one thing had become clear – it would not be possible to form a new Government without Dick Spring when the Dáil met on 14 December.

Spring was quick to seize on his new mandate, using it to argue that he would be seeking the office of Taoiseach. He received a boost from an unexpected source when Fine Gael's Austin Currie, during his acceptance speech in Dublin West, said he, too, agreed that Spring was the popular choice for Taoiseach. However, he withdrew the statement within a matter of hours.

From the moment the election results were concluded, Spring made it clear he would not be pushed into an early decision. By the first weekend he was already making it clear that there were major differences in policy with both Fine Gael and the PDs. He singled out privatisation as just one example. He said the State was now witnessing "new politics".

"I don't believe that it's as simple as saying that he who has the largest body of deputies will be Taoiseach."

In his final speech to the outgoing Dáil he had said he would never support some of the policies of Fianna Fáil, Fine Gael or the PDs. And that was when he had only 16 seats. Now he had 33.

The first obstacle came in early December when both Fine Gael and the PDs made it clear that they would not participate in any Government involving the Democratic Left party. Spring said that if an agreement was worked out with DL, then he would stick by it in the formation of any new Government.

Already John Bruton and Des O'Malley had met in what was described as a "cordial atmosphere". Spring, however, chose to begin his negotiations with the Democratic Left. Labour was represented by Deputy Brendan Howlin and Fergus Finlay, while the Democratic Left negotiators were Deputy Pat Rabbitte, and MEP Des Geraghty.

Rabbitte says they were a little surprised when approached by Spring for talks.

"I think it was part of a very careful strategy on Dick's part. But there may have been divided counsel on the Labour side. Ruairí Quinn and Barry Desmond never particularly wanted to initiate any discussions with Democratic Left."

Rabbitte argues that Spring did not want to leave himself exposed to doing business with John Bruton and Alan Dukes and as their allies Pat Cox and Michael McDowell of the PDs.

"He deliberately sought to do business with Democratic Left so that he would be roughly on the same equal footing. I think he also understood there could be negative consequences down the line from doing business with Fianna Fáil, because the mood at the time was that whatever Dick Spring got a mandate for, it wasn't to do business with Albert Reynolds."

The new Labour Parliamentary Party met in the Shelbourne Hotel on 1 December for the first time. Many had to introduce themselves to their comrades.

An upbeat Dick Spring told the deputies that he would not commit the party to a Government that did not have job creation, and a dynamic role for the public sector, as major priorities. Each of the 33 deputies spoke, and by consensus Dick Spring was given a free hand for his negotiations with other parties.

On Thursday, 4 December, Spring issued a statement saying

it was "inaccurate" to suggest that a "Rainbow Coalition," consisting of Fine Gael, Labour and the PDs, was the only option available. He again repeated his intent to negotiate an agreement with Democratic Left, after which he would meet the Fine Gael Leader.

"I find it astonishing that any responsible politician would choose unilaterally to reject an agreement that they have not seen, and a set of policy objectives they have never considered," he concluded.

However, the possibility of a Labour/Democratic Left/Fine Gael alliance received a severe blow on 4 December with the defeat of DL candidate Eric Byrne in Dublin South-Central where the count had dragged on for some days.

A change in attitude by Dick Spring was immediately noticeable as he agreed to meet the Fine Gael Leader before any agreement with Democratic Left was concluded.

They met in the Constitution Room of the Shelbourne Hotel on Sunday, 7 December, at 11am.

It was the Labour Party which had made all the arrangements and, according to John Bruton "We just went along with them".

The Fine Gael team were surprised, however, to find that a vast array of media had also been notified of the meeting by the Labour handlers. The meeting lasted 90 minutes and both Leaders emerged grim-faced, John Bruton particularly so.

"It was a very straight-talking meeting," recalls John Bruton. "We both said what we felt about how we might operate together and the difficulties there were likely to be."

But he denied reports at the time that the two had remained standing for the duration of the meeting.

Both Leaders said they would be reporting back to their respective parties, but, significantly, there were no definite plans for any future meetings.

Fine Gael senator and historian Maurice Manning agrees that the lack of trust between Bruton and Spring was a major stumbling-block to any progress:

"One of the things that is almost impossible to explain is the way in which the Leaders of Fine Gael and Labour didn't get together in the period after 1987.

"If we go back to 1977 when Garret FitzGerald became leader of Fine Gael, he consciously set out to establish a relationship between himself and Labour Leaders with frequent meetings, dinners, lunches. Each kept the other informed. There wasn't any sort of vicious personal competition, so that when it came to talking about a basis for Government, there was a trust already there.

"It is my view that within the 1983-87 Cabinet, perhaps Fine Gael was not as sensitive to Labour's individual identity as it might have been. This would not have been so of Garret FitzGerald, but it is a point so often made by Labour subsequently, that there is probably some truth to it, even though I wasn't aware of it at the time.

"Within that Cabinet, from all the accounts I have heard, both John Bruton and Alan Dukes were very vigorous intellectually in putting forward their point of view. Both tended to want to win the argument they were putting forward. Dick Spring was not quite as adept at arguing back, even when he felt he was right. Frequently he left the Cabinet feeling fairly bruised at the hands of either Alan Dukes or John Bruton. The result was an enmity that spilled right over into their time in Opposition, so that after 1987 there was no attempt at getting together, socially or otherwise, to see if there was some sort of common ground.

"I think the failure to build up any sort of relationship was ultimately responsible for the formation of the Fianna Fáil/Labour Government. Sometimes in politics, as in life, personal relationships are the most important, and when people can't get together when the chemistry is wrong, other reasons will be found for the failure to form a Government. Had Alan Dukes or John Bruton been closer to Dick Spring, or Dick Spring been closer to them, then the history of what happened after the 1992 general election might have been very different."

Manning also argues that a Government formed of Fine Gael, Labour, Democratic Left and Tony Gregory would not have survived six months.

"It couldn't have faced up to the huge crises and deputies would have been voting all over the place.

"A Government which included the Progressive Democrats probably wouldn't have lasted much longer because however much Labour distrusted Fine Gael, their distrust of the PDs, and in particular, people like Michael McDowell, was total. They regarded them as ideological purists who were setting out to privatise everything that moved in Ireland, and of wanting to impose a Reaganite or Thatcherite ideology. I don't think that would have been a very happy Government either."

Meanwhile, Fianna Fáil remained cleverly aloof from all discussions, in public at any rate, although it was later revealed that behind-the-scenes contacts had been made by Brian Lenihan and Bertie Ahern.

Brian first made contact with Ruairí Quinn, and when he signalled that Labour were interested in talking, Brian passed the word onto Albert Reynolds. From that point on, Bertie Ahern became the chief negotiator.

The talks between Labour and Democratic Left concluded with the publication of a working paper entitled: "Policy Proposals for a Government to build Social and Economic Justice in Ireland".

The document was general in nature and failed, for example,

to set down any firm guidelines on whether or not borrowing should adhere strictly to the Maastricht guidelines as argued by Fianna Fáil. All it stated was that the criteria in the Maastricht Treaty "are relevant".

The document contained the now familiar proposals for a National Economic and Social Forum, a new wider body to work in association with the NESF and an ambitious aim to reduce unemployment to 25,000 over a period of ten years. The idea of a State banking system was included and the proposed privatisation of the ICC and ACC was "cancelled".

It was also proposed that 4,000 new local authority houses be built every year.

There were proposals, too, in the area of social reform including the sale of contraceptives through vending machines, a referendum on divorce, and the de-criminalising of homosexuality.

Spring agreed with Democratic Left that he would not conclude any negotiations for Government with the other parties without first consulting with them. There was disagreement, however, between the two sides on policy on the North of Ireland, and this issue was left for later discussion, if there was to be a "later".

Meanwhile, the continuing refusal by Fine Gael to have any discussions with Democratic Left caused Fianna Fáil to start sending signals to Dick Spring that they were available for talks.

On 10 December, four days before the new Dáil was due to convene, Taoiseach Albert Reynolds sent a "position paper" to the Labour leader in response to the Labour/DL agreed proposals.

The document had been drafted by a number of Fianna Fáil advisers, notably Dr Martin Mansergh, during the previous week as a stand-by paper in response to the growing uncertainty of any outcome to the FG/Lab/PD talks.

Mr Reynolds specifically requested a meeting with Mr Spring upon his return from the Edinburgh summit.

In Edinburgh an upbeat Mr Reynolds told journalists it was "pretty certain" he would be Taoiseach "for some time to come".

Albert Reynolds returned from Edinburgh in the early hours of Sunday morning, 13 December. He agreed to a meeting with Dick Spring in the Berkeley Court Hotel later in the evening. The meeting lasted 90 minutes and afterwards both men told a packed foyer that it had been "constructive".

Spring refused to be drawn on whether he could form a Coalition with Fianna Fáil, saying such questions were "premature".

Having claimed to have secured a record £8 billion in EC funding in Edinburgh, Reynolds was full of confidence, as his handlers quickly dismissed any idea of a rotating Taoiseach.

Reynolds also revealed that he had called a meeting of all party Leaders for the following morning to try to agree a Ceann Comhairle for the new Dáil.

Meanwhile, the Fine Gael Front Bench also met in its party headquarters in Mount Street.

Addressing the Labour Party Annual Conference the following April in Waterford, Mr Spring claimed in his Leader's address that he had phoned John Bruton on the night of 13 December. He singled out the telephone call as particularly significant.

"In that conversation (which was short) I told him that unless he was prepared to change his view and to agree to the inclusion of Democratic Left in negotiations, in order to achieve a more balanced structure, I would be unwilling to recommend taking negotiations with Fine Gael and the Progressive Democrats any further."

According to Spring, John Bruton refused to drop any of the pre-conditions he had imposed on the negotiations.

"That was the moment the die was cast," declared Spring. "Every time I have to listen to Fine Gael carping and moaning since, I remember that moment."

John Bruton, however, rejects that any such telephone conversation took place.

Bruton keeps a diary of all his meetings and calls in simple copy-books which he regularly consults. No such conversation is recorded in his notes for Sunday, 13 December.

Bruton says he "didn't bother" to watch Dick Spring's Waterford address on television, but was annoyed when he read the reports on the Sunday papers.

"First, I had no conversation of any kind with Mr Spring on that day," he says.

"Second, I did have a telephone conversation on Monday, 14 December, at around 7pm. According to my notes Mr Spring said he was about to go into a meeting of his Parliamentary Party. He asked if Fine Gael would agree to rotate the office of Taoiseach with him. I said we had decided we would not. At that point Mr Spring said he would 'have to do' what he would 'have to do' (or words to that effect). At no point in this conversation did he ask about including Democratic Left in negotiations."

According to Pat Rabbitte, Democratic Left were sceptical about Fine Gael's insistence that they would not do business with them. But a harder line developed when people like Peter Barry started to press it.

John Bruton says the only reason for Fine Gael's position was the so-called "Moscow money", a reference to news reports that The Workers' Party had received financial aid from the discredited Soviet communist regime. Proinsias De Rossa has always denied these reports.

"We had made it clear," says Pat Rabbitte, "that we did not see much point in being in a Government that would involve a four-party Coalition, nor did we see much point in being in a Government that included Fianna Fáil, not least from the point of view of being numerically redundant. So, effectively, it was

Fine Gael with whom business would have to be done."

All five party Leaders met in the Taoiseach's office on 14 December to discuss the issue of the Ceann Comhairle.

The previous evening Albert Reynolds told Dick Spring he would be nominating Brian Lenihan for the post. Spring replied that in that case he would be nominating Liam Kavanagh.

On Monday morning they agreed to nominate Seán Treacy, the outgoing Ceann Comhairle.

When the Dáil met later that day Albert Reynolds was nominated for Taoiseach by Fianna Fáil, but was defeated. So too was John Bruton (supported by the PDs), and Dick Spring (supported by Democratic Left).

Mr O'Malley's speech on the nomination of a Taoiseach is regarded as another significant turning point in the ending of the rainbow idea.

In a hard-hitting attack on the Labour Party he said they had done well only because they had "carefully ditched their former political baggage".

The people had not elected a socialist orLeft Government, he claimed, and less than a quarter of the members of the Dáil came from what they call "the Left".

O'Malley's vehemence took many of the Labour Party deputies by surprise.

"There was," said one of them, "the sound of a door closing."

The Dáil adjourned for eight days and Reynolds went to Áras an Uachtaráin to resign as Taoiseach. He then continued in office as acting Taoiseach along with the other members of the Cabinet.

That night, the 33 members of the Labour Parliamentary Party met and having reviewed the situation, agreed to allow Mr Spring to enter serious negotiations with Fianna Fáil.

The talks got under way with two teams of three on each side. The Fianna Fáil negotiators were Bertie Ahern, Brian Cowen and

Noel Dempsey, while Dick Spring nominated Ruairí Quinn, Mervyn Taylor and Brendan Howlin. A news blackout was agreed to, and the negotiations got under way on the basis of policy statements. The make-up of the Cabinet was to be a matter for discussion between the two party Leaders, if a final document could be hammered out.

Overshadowing the talks, however, was the up-coming appearance by Dick Spring at the Beef Tribunal. Although confirming that he would not be revealing the identity of those who supplied him with information, Mr Spring insisted that he would be totally forthright in his evidence, much of which had been critical of the Fianna Fáil Government of 1987 to 1989, which included Albert Reynolds.

Until the European election in 1989, it was Barry Desmond who had made most of the running for Labour on the beef controversy. However, when Desmond left for Europe, Spring himself took over the attack, an indication of how seriously the party viewed the issue.

In particular, Spring had been critical of the relationship between Fianna Fáil and Larry Goodman.

Among other allegations, he had claimed:

1. Goodman International received "favourable treatment" from Fianna Fáil within weeks of its return to office in 1987 as evidenced by the granting of export credit insurance and a major IDA-backed development plan.
2. The granting of the export credit insurance was contrary to the best advice available to the Government – a direct attack on Albert Reynolds.
3. That Mr Reynolds' decisions in relation to export credit insurance proved to be "disastrous" from the point of view of the beef industry.

4. That while all this support was being given, the Fraud Squad was being asked to investigate irregularities at Goodman plants in Waterford and Ballymun, and a Goodman associate, Nobby Quinn, was being prosecuted and convicted for the fraudulent use of forged customs stamps.

Dick Spring took the witness stand in Dublin Castle on Monday, 21 December. His evidence was, in many respects, more marked by its omissions than its contents. The most notable absence were the two words "Albert Reynolds".

Much of his evidence was vague due to two impending High Court actions concerning parliamentary privilege and the refusal to reveal sources.

Spring then proceeded to deal with fact only, excluding matters of hearsay and comment.

This drew the embarrassing remark from the chairman, Mr Justice Liam Hamilton:

"The reality is that you have no evidence, good, bad or indifferent," to give to the Tribunal.

"I accept that," replied Spring.

Contrary to normal practice, Spring was not led through his evidence and therefore, did not have the opportunity to outline his allegations.

His cross-examination by counsel for the Attorney General and the State, Henry Hickey SC, was also remarkably low-key. Mr Hickey also acted for Reynolds at the Tribunal.

Spring made it clear that he was standing over his allegations, but the effect of the day's proceedings was that no direct conflict arose between him and Albert Reynolds. A dangerous bend had been rounded.

Summing up in *The Irish Times* journalist Fintan O'Toole

concluded: "In the end, none of Spring's evidence is likely to have added greatly to the sum total of the Tribunal's knowledge of the matters under investigation. But then, the significance of the evidence of Mr Spring was always more likely to lie in its possible political repercussions than in the revelation of any substantial new facts."

When Larry Goodman himself subsequently gave evidence to the Tribunal on 12 March, he said he was "just appalled that a person of Mr Spring's eminence and calibre" would make such allegations "about an Irish person or company that had been in business successfully for more than 39 years".

In evidence before the Tribunal on 5 March, a former Goodman financial director, Brian Britton, claimed he was used by Dick Spring in the initial row over irregularities at two of the group's plants.

He said the then Labour TD, Barry Desmond, had raised the issue in the Dáil in March 1989, claiming that £20 million in export refunds had been withheld from the Goodman group. He had also referred to a £2 million or £3 million fraud.

Both of these allegations were completely untrue, and remained so, he said.

Mr Britton said that on 14 March, after Mr Desmond's allegations, he received a telephone call from Dick Spring.

"He told me he was very annoyed about the comments being made by the company, and by me in particular," said Mr Britton.

He said Mr Spring had told him he had a letter from the Department of Agriculture to the company in January imposing a fine of £1.08 million. Britton said he was unaware of a fine and he agreed with Spring that he would check it out. He added that the Labour Leader assured him that if the letter was genuine, the company would not hear any more about it that night. They were to exchange calls the following morning.

However, that same evening Mr Britton received a call from

the company's public relations representative, who told him that Barry Desmond was claiming in the Dáil that his allegations were substantiated by a letter in his possession.

"I subsequently realised that Dick Spring had used the telephone call to give credence to the letter," he said.

****

Having escaped the potentially lethal trap door of the Beef Tribunal, the negotiations between Fianna Fáil and Labour continued.

When the Dáil met for the second time on 23 December, Spring reported progress. He had, he said, detected a desire for fundamental change during his discussions with Fianna Fáil.

But he could not guarantee that the negotiations would be successfully concluded.

"The Government that will be formed after these negotiations," he told the Dáil, "will be a Government that presides over a return to the highest standards of public life – and unless and until the Labour Party is satisfied that that is going to be the case, the Labour Party will be concluding no agreement.

"It will also be a Government, if it is to include the Labour Party, that will preside over the emergence of a new order of social priorities in Ireland. Those on the margins will be included, those who have no voice will be given a voice – that is the only kind of Government that matters to us."

The Dáil adjourned again for the Christmas recess without electing a Taoiseach.

On 31 December the *Irish Press* revealed that Dick Spring's price for a partnership Government with Fianna Fáil was Tánaiste and Minister for Foreign Affairs.

Labour sources let it be known that the difference in numbers with Fianna Fáil did not make the idea of a rotating Taoiseach a realistic possibility, but Spring would be seeking what was regarded as the next best thing, and six full Cabinet Ministers.

As Minister for Foreign Affairs, Spring would be demanding responsibility for Anglo-Irish affairs.

The news sent shock waves through the back-benches of Fianna Fáil, but nobody complained very loudly. It had long become obvious that if this Government was not formed, another general election was inevitable, and Fianna Fáil certainly did not want that.

David Andrews made no secret of the fact that he wished to keep the prestigious Foreign Affairs portfolio where he had made a considerable impact, but confirmed his acceptance of whatever decision the Taoiseach would make.

A key factor in the progress of the talks was the excellent relationship that developed between the two senior negotiators, Ruairí Quinn and Bertie Ahern. This resulted in a smooth flow of discussions and only a relatively small number of matters were referred back to the Leaders for resolution.

The main stumbling block was the budget, with Labour eventually having to concede that the final decisions could only be made in the context of a full partnership Government because of the requirement of Cabinet confidentiality.

The Dáil reconvened on 5 January but the only announcement made by the Taoiseach was the re-assignment of Padraig Flynn's Justice portfolio (he had been appointed EC Commissioner) to Maire Geoghegan-Quinn. The House then adjourned for one week to January 12.

Meanwhile, contingency plans were already in place for a special Labour Party conference on Sunday, 10 January to consider the partnership plan.

However, there was to be one final hurdle, set by the PDs.

In the week in which both the FF and Labour Parliamentary Parties met, Des O'Malley went to Dick Spring and claimed that a barrister on the State's legal team had tried to intimidate one of his counsel in the Horse Shoe bar of the Shelbourne Hotel. The barrister had also claimed to have seen some of the preparatory notes in O'Malley's private files on the Tribunal.

The Attorney General, Harry Whelehan, held an immediate meeting with the State team and concluded, there was no evidence to support the claim that any private notes had been illegally intercepted. The Bar Council, however, initiated its own inquiry.

Dick Spring reacted first by stating he could not go into Government with Fianna Fáil "if there are clouds hanging about", but concluded that there was no need to halt his discussions.

On Thursday, 7 January, both the Fianna Fáil and Labour Parliamentary Parties met to approve the Programme for Government.

On 8 January both Dick Spring and Albert Reynolds met for several hours to resolve outstanding problems concerning the budget and the Cabinet make-up. However, final decisions on the details of the Cabinet positions were postponed until the following Monday, the day after Labour's special conference.

21

LIVING WITH THE IN-LAWS

Sunday, 10 January 1993, saw 1,200 Labour delegates crowd into the National Concert Hall in Dublin's Earlsfort Terrace. It also saw Dick Spring in a particularly good mood.

An opinion poll published that morning showed the party a full seven points up on its record high of 19 per cent in the November general election.

Proposing the motion to give the go-ahead for a deal with Fianna Fáil, Spring again repeated the importance of trust in the new Government and the determination to conform to "the highest standards of accountability".

He said that during the election campaign he had made it clear that Labour would insist that any negotiations it had with other parties would be conducted on a basis of partnership, or not at all. Only one party, Fianna Fáil, had taken that determination seriously.

"The same people who predicted that we didn't have what it takes before the election are saying it again. They are saying that we haven't got the skills, the political experience, the commitment or strength to bring about the changes we promised to fight for," he told the delegates.

The man who seconded the motion, Emmet Stagg, had often been a controversial figure in the past. Now he was tame as a lamb.

During the previous year he had left the Labour Party over the Leader's failure to spell out exactly where he stood on Coalition.

For a time he toyed with joining Democratic Left but, in the end, he re-joined Labour.

Stagg now told the delegates that back in 1986 the party had set a ten-year target aimed at the level of strength where it would properly be prepared to go into Government. But that target had already been well exceeded, he claimed.

There were a few dissenting voices.

"There's a man here from Mullinavat," Paddy Costello, a South Kilkenny delegate told the conference, "who says that when you lie down with dogs, you get up with fleas."

The dogs in question were Fianna Fáil, but Paddy Costello's words were not sufficient to prevent a massive endorsement of the proposed Coalition.

One young delegate, Joe French, reminded the conference that it was Dick Spring's own assertion that Fianna Fáil had dragged politics into the gutter. More than a mere cloud, a hurricane, hung over Albert's head, he claimed.

But it was a regal-like Dick Spring who looked down on the forest of hands holding blue cards aloft to endorse the proposed partnership.

"Come on the Kingdom," shouted one Kerry delegate.

Another delegate from Drogheda, summed up the meeting: "The rainbow has passed, let the Spring rain begin."

That evening, Kerry-born writer Con Houlihan met some of his country men on their way home. He said he had never seen such triumphalism since Kerry won the All-Ireland Final in 1975.

"It mystified me," he wrote later. "I felt like the small boy who couldn't see the emperor's new suit; I felt that perhaps it was my myopia – and the emperor had a new suit after all."

In his speech Dick Spring said there would be no honeymoon for the new Government. Later Fergus Finlay would recall that Labour had been granted only one honeymoon day, the Sunday afternoon in the National Concert Hall.

The 58-page Programme for a Partnership Government contained many of the original proposals in the document agreed with Democratic Left. While much of the language was of a very general nature, such as committing the new regime to worthy aims like greater social equality and a better distribution of resources, there were a number of concrete proposals.

Included was a commitment to creating a Third Banking Force by merging the ICC and the ACC; the setting up of a National Economic and Social Forum (NESF); and the establishment of a jobs fund to a future level of £750 million.

In Government reform there were plans for an Ethics Bill, four new Standing Committees, and plans to introduce State funding for political parties. However, the Labour Party demand for a Minister for the Handicapped had been dropped.

On the social front there were plans to begin the construction of 3,500 local authority houses in 1993; to increase child benefit allowances and to tackle the major problem of hospital waiting lists.

There was a commitment to introduce divorce legislation by 1994 and homosexuality was to be de-criminalised in line with the European Convention on Human Rights.

Under its agreement with Democratic Left, the Labour Party was obliged to consult with that party before entering any arrangement for Government. However, as Democratic Left had already indicated they were not interested in any association with Fianna Fáil, the issue was dealt with by way of a brief telephone conversation.

It was a tense Dáil that met on 12 January to elect Albert Reynolds as Taoiseach by the biggest majority ever, 102 votes to 60.

Reynolds announced the establishment of five new Government departments and a series of major structural reforms.

Labour got six senior ministries which necessitated the dropping of two out-going Fianna Fáil Ministers – Dr John O'Connell, who had indicated he did not wish to be considered again, and Séamus Brennan, who had been Minister for Education.

A new office of Tánaiste was to be set up in Government Buildings where Mr Spring, in addition to being Tánaiste, would monitor the implementation of the Programme for Government. He would be assisted by a Minister of State, Eithne Fitzgerald.

Ruairí Quinn was named as the Minister in the new Department of Employment and Enterprise, Mervyn Taylor in Equality and Law Reform, Michael D Higgins in Arts, Culture and the Gaeltacht, Niamh Bhreathnach in Education, and Brendan Howlin in Health.

It was a significant achievement for Spring. Never before had there been such a re-definition of the senior ministries and the creation of so many new portfolios.

While Ruairí Quinn was technically taking over the old Department of Industry, it was obvious that the new Department of Employment and Enterprise would have a different emphasis.

Niamh Bhreathnach, a former teacher, was to be the first Labour Minister for Education, while Brendan Howlin was an interesting choice for Health, always a contentious area.

Michael D Higgins was a most popular choice for Arts, Culture and the Gaeltacht and despite Des O'Malley's humorous claim that he "would go mad in Government", Higgins was seen as an ideal Minister, and a well-deserved winner.

But it was the creation of the new Department of Equality and Law Reform that caused most interest. Lawyer Mervyn Taylor would have responsibility for much of the progressive social legislation in the new Government, including the preparation and introduction of divorce laws.

In the run-up to the partnership it had been freely predicted that former Attorney General and close Spring confidante, John Rogers, would be re-appointed to the office. Oddly, however, Rogers was not on the team, and the out-going incumbent, Harry Whelehan, remained.

The Taoiseach and Tánaiste did not lose much time in appointing their Junior Ministers, and their names and portfolios were revealed on 14 January.

Labour got five posts – Emmet Stagg, at the Department of the Environment, with responsibility for Housing and Urban renewal; Gerry O'Sullivan, at the Department of the Marine, with responsibility for Port Development, Safety and Inland Waterways; Brian O'Shea, at the Department of Agriculture, with special responsibility for Food and Horticulture; Eithne Fitzgerald, at the office of Tánaiste and the Department of Finance, with responsibility for the National Development Plan; and Joan Burton, at the Department of Social Welfare, with responsibility for Poverty, and the Integration of the Tax and Social Welfare Codes.

Overall, it was an innovative, if somewhat surprising, choice of ministries. Spring had clearly opted for youth rather than experience.

There were a number of obvious omissions, most notably Liam Kavanagh who had served in the 1983-87 Coalition. Neither was the experienced deputy, from Carlow/Kilkenny, Séamus Pattison, included. He had been the party's standard-bearer for many years and had served as a Junior Minister. No place was found either for South Tipperary Michael Ferris, who had been tipped as a Junior Minister.

But perhaps the most surprising omission of all was Jim Kemmy, the former Democratic Socialist from Limerick. Kemmy had been hotly tipped for the Cabinet but did not even make it to the junior ranks.

Kemmy's agreement to join Labour had given the party a huge boost, and had made it the biggest party on Limerick Corporation. Furthermore, his influence had gone a long way towards almost securing a second seat for the party in East Limerick.

It was difficult, for example, to understand why Emmet Stagg had made it over the head of Jim Kemmy. Stagg readily admits there were people whom he believed were ahead of him in the queue for Ministerial office.

Spring moved quickly to ease the pain of disappointment by appointing Kemmy as chairman of the party, Toddy O'Sullivan as chairman of the Parliamentary Party and Michael Ferris as chief whip. The back-benchers moved to appoint their own committee of 22, which was, however, approved by the establishment.

There was some feeling among the back-benchers that some of the posts obtained by Labour, such as Arts, Culture and Equality, were more suitable for Junior Ministers. They also felt the Labour negotiators "took their eye off the ball" in letting the EC Commissionership, the posts of Attorney General, Ceann Comhairle and Leas Ceann-Comhairle, all slip out of their hands. However, in early September, Dick Spring demanded and secured the post of Member of the European Court of Auditors for MEP Barry Desmond. The post carries a salary of £162,000 per annum.

There was also some resentment at a letter Spring sent to all back-benchers to explain why he was not able to appoint them to Ministerial posts. Long-serving TDs got the same letter as those elected for the first time, and this caused some hurt.

Once elected to office, the new Government quickly made it clear that there would be a new style of Government. Each Minister was to appoint his or her own Partnership Programme Manager. All of these would meet on a weekly basis to sort out minor difficulties in implementing the Programme for Government and clear the way for Cabinet meetings.

Labour Ministers also quickly appointed a number of special advisers, many of whom had been former party activists.

Spring's own office of Tánaiste was costed at an additional charge to the Exchequer of £600,000. It was set up with a staff of 16, headed by a civil servant, Julie O'Neill, at Assistant Secretary rank. The Book of Estimates, published on 17 February, showed the total cost of the office at £831,000. However, £231,000 of this was attributed to spending that would have occurred in any event.

But the appointments, handled badly by the Government, drew immediate and intense criticism from the Opposition.

PD leader, Des O'Malley, claimed Spring was trying to establish himself as a "semi-rival Taoiseach", a move, he claimed, which was contrary to the Constitution.

It emerged that Mr Spring had investigated the possibility of having a Tánaiste's Question Time in the Dáil, as distinct from his Dáil Question Time, in his role as Minister for Foreign Affairs. Spring had thought that he could open up his new office of Tánaiste to parliamentary scrutiny on matters relating to his own department, such as the National Development Plan, the new National Economic and Social Forum and his implementation of the Programme for Government. However, the Standing Orders of the Dáil, drawn up in 1986, made no provision for the office of Tánaiste.

"I have been looking at the Constitution," said Mr O'Malley, "which does not allow for such an activity, and the only reference to the Tánaiste is that he will substitute for the Taoiseach while the Taoiseach is absent."

The early days of the new Government were marked by a great deal of confusion about the division of responsibilities. Nowhere was it more highlighted than in the case of the Interpretative Centre at Mullaghmore, Co Clare. It was unclear whether responsibility for this controversial development fell under the control of Junior Fianna Fáil Minister Noel Dempsey, who was in charge of the Office of Public Works, or the new Labour Minister for the Arts, Culture and the Gaeltacht, Michael D Higgins.

New to partnership Government, Spring quickly surrounded himself with a close band of trusted advisers. No one had been closer in the past than his right hand man and chief wordsmith, Fergus Finlay. A former trade union official and main trouble shooter, Finlay once said the reason he was indispensable to Dick Spring was because he could write 300 words on any given topic in 20 minutes.

Finlay had been Assistant Government Press Secretary in the 1983 Coalition, and now wished to move on from that role. He was appointed a special adviser to the Tánaiste and programme manager in the Department of Foreign Affairs.

Spring appointed Greg Sparks, a partner in the Dublin accountancy firm, Farrell Grant Sparks, as Labour's chief partnership programme manager.

The Tánaiste also appointed his former personal secretary, Sally Clarke, to his new office in Government Buildings. In, too, came Greencore economist Willy Scally and young barrister Finbarr O'Malley.

Mr Scally had long associations with the Labour Party. He was involved in negotiations for the formation of the Fine Gael/Labour Coalition Government under Garret FitzGerald, and had previously served as an economic adviser to Dick Spring.

Junior Counsel Finbarr O'Malley represented Labour Party interests at the Tribunal of Inquiry into the Beef Industry. His brother, Chris O'Malley, served for a time as a Fine Gael MEP. He had devilled at the Bar with PD deputy, Michael McDowell.

The Tánaiste's sister, Kerry Councillor Maeve Spring, continued on as his constituency assistant, although he caused some confusion when he referred to her by her married name, Maeve Sweeney.

Speaking in the Dáil on 10 February, he said: "It is my intention to appoint ... Ms Maeve Sweeney as constituency personal assistant."

Finally, Spring appointed *Irish Independent* political reporter John Foley, a regular golfing partner, as Assistant Government Press Secretary. He later succeeded long-time Reynolds aide, Bart Cronin, as Head of the Government Information Services.

Ruairí Quinn, now Minister for Employment and Enterprise, appointed a UCD lecturer, Dr Frank Roche, as his programme manager. His task was to concentrate on the development of indigenous industry.

Mervyn Taylor appointed another UCD lecturer, Richard Humphries, as his special adviser. Ironically, Humphries had once written an article in a magazine detailing methods of parliamentary obstruction. Taylor also appointed the chairman of the Labour Party in his constituency, Paul Mulhern, as his programme manager.

In Health, the new Minister, Brendan Howlin, appointed Anne Byrne as his programme manager. She was a long-time employee of the Labour Party and was a key figure in his election campaigns in Wexford. As special adviser he appointed a medical doctor, Dr Tim Collins. Dr Collins had formerly worked as an adviser on the environment to Mary Harney when she was a Minister of State. He was a Labour supporter, and was mentioned as a possible candidate in the November 1992 election in the Wicklow constituency.

Education Minister Niamh Bhreathnach appointed the principal of Monkstown CBS in her own Dún Laoghaire constituency, Pat Keating, as her principal adviser. His main task was to take charge of the then up-coming White Paper on

Education. As programme manager she appointed James Wrynne, the former treasurer of the Labour Party. He had worked as a lecturer in business policy in the Dublin College of Marketing and Design.

Ms Bhreathnach also appointed former Labour Party Assistant Press Officer, Sineaid Bruton, as her personal press officer in Marlborough St. However, the Minister hit the headlines with the appointment of her daughter, Cliodhna Ferris, as her constituency secretary. The Minister fought back saying her daughter had always helped in her office in Dún Laoghaire, and was now earning a meagre salary of £11,000 per annum.

In all, the Government sanctioned the appointment of some 135 staff at a cost to the taxpayer of £3 million per year.

In their appointments the Labour Party had chosen almost exclusively from outside the ranks of the civil service.

Referring to the appointment of a "record number of relations, friends and political cronies" to salaried positions, Fine Gael deputy, Alan Shatter compared the new Labour administration to the reign of Caligula, the Roman emperor, who had appointed his horse to the Senate.

"It is probably fortunate that the Government some years ago abolished Bord na gCapall and that the Tánaiste does not own a horse," he said. "If he did, there would be a serious risk of him being appointed to chair that defunct body."

The appointments also drew the wrath of the media.

Writing in the *Irish Press*, Emily O'Reilly noted that not one of the posts had been publicly advertised.

"There was no vetting procedure, no opportunity for a neutral group to decide whether the taxpayer should be asked to pay for the services of these people.

"Those in the Tánaiste's office are Dick Spring's private property. He chose them. He will issue them with their job briefs.

They will work to his interests alone. Yet we are paying their wages."

O'Reilly and others argued that the civil service was full of expert, skilled people who were well capable of running any Government department.

"Politically the whole thing has backfired in Spring's face," wrote O'Reilly. "It's been a massive PR blunder from which Labour will take a long time to recover. Whatever about the reality, the public perception is of nepotism, croneyism, jobs for the boys and girls on an outrageous scale."

Democratic Left deputy Pat Rabbitte agrees the appointment of the advisers was handled "appallingly badly". Said Rabbitte: "What might have turned out to be a good experiment in using advisers was undermined by the blatant family strokes that were engaged for other posts. I also think it's not clear in all cases that it was expert advice rather than compensating loyal constituency supporters that was the criterion."

The wrath of the media continued, with the most scathing piece penned by controversial journalist and former soccer player, Eamon Dunphy, in the *Sunday Independent* on 28 February.

In a full page article, Dunphy accused Spring of betraying the Irish people. He said the new Tánaiste had been "playing games" in the formation of a Government while the country had endured a severe currency crisis and when a computer factory in Galway, Digital, announced the loss of over 1,000 jobs.

Dunphy ended his tirade with the following comment: "Mr Spring should never visit Galway again ... The Minister for Foreign Affairs should spend as much time as he can abroad. He is a disgrace to his country and, to borrow a phrase from Brendan Behan: 'A bollocks of the highest order'."

Never before had the Tánaiste of a country been subjected to such verbal abuse in a newspaper.

Dunphy's over-reaction backfired in that it caused some sympathy for Spring, whose popularity was already slipping from public grasp.

For a while Spring hinted that he might take legal action, but in the end, did not. "I read it all, and decided it was beneath contempt," he said later.

Spring did, however, react vigorously to an article written by freelance journalist John Cooney in the *Irish Independent* on 4 March. (Spring and Cooney had had an altercation in Leinster House in November 1989.)

In his article Cooney argued that Spring had "broken free" from his role as Tánaiste and Labour Leader into a new role as international statesman. He cited visits by Spring to Warsaw, Budapest and an interview on BBC television.

Cooney pointed out that while Spring was out of the country, the visiting President of the European Parliament, Egon Klepsch, had to be looked after by Spring's understudy, Fianna Fáil's Tom Kitt.

He also argued that the Tánaiste appeared to be less informed about the horrific details of incest and brutality imposed on a 27-year-old Kilkenny woman by her English father than he was about sexual abuses against Bosnian women.

"What is not in doubt is the public relations strategy to launch Mr Spring as a statesman operating at a level superior to the time-warped and border-snooping Fianna Fáilers, led by Rip Van Reynolds," he concluded.

Two days later Spring's reply in the letters page began: "Wrong, wrong, wrong. And viciously so. This is the only description that I can possibly apply to yesterday's article by John Cooney, which attempted to carry on the campaign of smear and sneer that has permeated the Independent Group's coverage of the Labour Party since the formation of the Government."

Spring accused Cooney of making a "crude political point" in comparing the Bosnian women to the horrific incest case in Kilkenny. He dismissed Cooney's claims of trying to distance himself from the Labour Party as "vicious and unfounded rubbish".

Cooney replied to Spring's letter saying that he was surprised that he was so "thin-skinned" as to resort to a feeble letter to the editor.

An *Independent* reader, Kevin McPhillips, from Dublin, describing Spring's letter as "amazingly crude and venomous", questioned the Labour Leader's fitness for high public office.

Now in a writing mood, Spring penned a second defence of his actions in his local *Kerryman* newspaper on Friday, 5 March.

"Nothing means more to me than the integrity of the Labour Party," he began. "If ever I felt I had done anything to damage the integrity of the party, I would willingly walk away from public life."

The Tánaiste explained that what he had tried to do was to put a structure in place that would bring about fundamental and lasting change in Ireland.

"With my own expert draughtsman and legal adviser, I can bring Bills to Government in a completed form, and short-circuit many of the delays that have always held up reform," he said.

His new Office of Tánaiste was not, he wrote, "some fancy office block," but rather a number of spare rooms in the Taoiseach's Department.

"It's new and it's different," he said, "but it is far from corrupt. In fact it offers an opportunity to put a total commitment to work on solving problems."

And there was a special word for his sister, Maeve:

"Everyone who knows her knows of her dedication and commitment... She deals with pain and hardship every day – and she does it with tact and compassion. How anyone could believe that I should get rid of Maeve because I became a Minister is beyond belief."

For a time, scarcely a day passed without some criticism of Dick Spring in the newspapers. Fellow county man Con Houlihan took up the topic in his "Tributaries" column in the *Evening Press*.

The new Government, he said, resembled the Spanish Armada, an expedition that had been seriously wounded before it left the harbour and therefore came to little good.

On the question of appointments, Houlihan said they did "no good to the Labour Party; not alone should it be above corruption, it should be seen to be above corruption... This array of appointments was a tactical error."

Houlihan argued that the decision to go into Government with Fianna Fáil was potentially lethal.

"When Labour coalesced with Fianna Fáil, they betrayed the hopes of that element which provided the yeast last November."

He concluded by warning of a rift with the party:

"I know a few deputies who feel marginalised. They suspect that too much influence is being wielded by people outside the Parliamentary Party."

22
TIGHT-ROPE WALKER

March 5, 1993. The venue, the Mansion House on Dublin's Dawson St. It was there that the newly appointed Tánaiste and Minister for Foreign Affairs, Dick Spring, decided to make his first major speech on Northern Ireland.

The speech had been heavily flagged for weeks, to such an extent that it had caused major concern among Fianna Fáil back-benchers that a new initiative on Northern Ireland was about to be unveiled. In the Cabinet make-up Spring had asked for, and had been granted, full responsibility for matters concerning Northern Ireland. The move represented a watershed in Irish politics where the Taoiseach of the day had always retained overall responsibility for the North.

Nobody had zealously guarded this role more closely than Charles Haughey, who retained tight control over every syllable that was uttered on this sensitive topic.

But Dick Spring had insisted on change in Irish politics. Not just change in domestic politics, but change in attitude to Northern Ireland.

He had, himself, come from a strong Republican tradition in North Kerry. His father, Dan Spring, had argued strongly against the execution of the IRA chief-of-staff, Charlie Kerins, in the 1940s.

North Kerry, it could be argued, is one of the strongest Republican constituencies in the country. When Dick Spring first entered the Dáil in the summer of 1981, he relied heavily on H-Block transfers to secure his election.

But throughout his political career Spring was careful to adopt a very moderate line, and to strongly oppose violence of all kinds.

Back in December 1982, once given a mandate to go into Coalition with Fine Gael, Spring immediately took the opportunity to call for an all-party consensus in the Republic on the North.

It was high time, he said, to get away from the "history book mentality and the Civil War politics" which had been practised by politicians for so long.

"We have to respect all traditions in Northern Ireland, and given the serious downswing in relation to these issues in the last few months and the escalation in violence, Northern Ireland is a very sensitive area and the approach must be sympathetic," he emphasised.

From the outset he made it clear that he would have no truck with the men of violence, and that he would not meet any deputations which included members of Sinn Féin. He would, he said, support the "complete isolation of anyone who supports the violent and murderous methods of the paramilitaries".

But he cautioned against proscribing such groups.

Speaking at a Labour Party meeting in Dublin in June 1984, he said his reason for this was that by keeping "the political avenues open to them as long as it is possible to do so", he hoped that at some time they would "renounce murder as a means of achieving their ends".

Secondly he did not wish to be party to any action which might possibly have the effect of increasing the "romantic" appeal of those who supported murder.

"It is morally impossible," he declared, "to carry an Armalite in one hand and a ballot box in the other."

He led his party's team at the New Ireland Forum where he

had difficulty in keeping unity among his members. Senator Mary Robinson vehemently opposed committing the Forum to a unitary state model.

It was, for example, Spring, who came up with the wording "proposals" instead of "suggestions" for the notions of federal, confederal or joint authority models in the final report. Spring and members of the Labour Party had argued that the word "suggestions" had downgraded these ideas as solutions to the Northern Ireland situation.

The Forum had marked an unprecedented episode in the history of Irish politics. Over a period of eleven months, the three main political parties in the Republic along with the SDLP in the North had met on almost 100 occasions, including over 50 Leaders' meetings, to establish an impressive degree of common ground on the most divisive national issue.

Former Minister for Foreign Affairs Peter Barry recalls Spring carving out his own path at the Forum.

"Dick Spring was not long elected leader when the Forum commenced," he recalls, "and he knew there were a lot of people in that room in Dublin Castle who were far more experienced than he was. Yet he refused to be over-influenced by some of his own delegates such as Mary Robinson and Frank Cluskey who were strongly pushing for a finer balancing towards the Unionist population."

Later Spring was not slow to criticise the then British Prime Minister, Margaret Thatcher, for her "inadequate" response to the Forum report. (He attended the Chequers talks where Mrs Thatcher made her infamous "out...out...out" remarks).

Addressing the party's annual conference in Cork in April 1985, he called on the British Prime Minister to show more courage and imagination in future negotiations.

"They (the British Government) could do the people of this

country an enormous service if they now addressed themselves seriously to the Northern question," he said.

Along with Garret FitzGerald and Peter Barry, Dick Spring was closely involved in the rounds of negotiations leading to the signing of the Anglo-Irish Agreement.

These negotiations made Spring a security risk.

Later, when he left Government, it was confirmed that he had received a number of death threats from the Provisional IRA during his four years as Tánaiste.

In January 1987, following his resignation from Government, the Department of Justice re-allocated him a State car and a Special Branch driver because of these threats.

Back in Opposition Dick Spring regularly made key speeches on Northern Ireland issues.

However, in a surprise speech in New York in July 1988, he unexpectedly called for the suspension of the Anglo-Irish Conference, while demanding a pledge from the Unionists on a commitment to power-sharing with the minority population.

The suggestion of a suspension of the Conference had first been mooted within a year of the signing as a means to draw Unionists into negotiations. But in an interview in the summer of 1986 with the *Belfast Telegraph*, Mrs Thatcher said she would regard a suspension of the working of the Agreement as a breach of the Agreement.

Spring's New York call drew a barrage of criticism on the Labour Leader from all sides, but the Official Unionist leader, James Molyneux, hailed it as evidence of a new "realism" in Dublin.

SDLP deputy leader Séamus Mallon described the proposal as "midsummer madness", while former Coalition colleague Peter Barry accused Spring of encouraging the Unionists to "keep pushing until they get rid of the whole agreement".

The then spokesperson for the Progressive Democrats, newly

elected Dáil deputy Geraldine Kennedy (now political correspondent with *The Irish Times*) said she fundamentally disagreed "with the ill-judged and immature proposal" by Mr Spring.

In the spring of 1991, Spring launched a new initiative on the North when he called on the Fianna Fáil/PD Coalition to be prepared to change Articles 2 and 3 of the Irish Constitution in favour of an aspiration claim.

The removal or re-wording of the Articles has been at the centre of all Anglo-Irish relations, and Spring's attitude to them was to become a source of major concern in the early part of the new 1993 Government.

Speaking in advance of the inter-party talks initiative by Northern Ireland Secretary, Sir Peter Brooke, in April 1991, Dick Spring said the Government would have to make concessions "in substance and in style" to the Unionists which went beyond Articles 2 and 3.

"The Proclamation of 1916," he said, " called for a society in Ireland based on civil and religious liberty – and if, in the process of these negotiations, our Government was in a position to say explicitly that they were willing to countenance the development of a truly pluralist and libertarian constitution, capable of encompassing the whole island as much as any small part of it, it would revolutionise the atmosphere in which those talks are likely to take place."

However, by January 1992, Spring was calling on the British Labour Party Leader, Neil Kinnock, to make a "major statement" on Northern Ireland in advance of the British general election as a move against a Unionist veto on all progress there.

In a letter to Kinnock, Spring quoted British Labour Party policy, as published in 1988, and asked for its reiteration in a major statement.

That policy stated: "While consent must, by definition, be freely given, no group or party will be allowed to exercise a veto on policies designed to win consent for unification. We do not believe it is responsible or adequate to await passively the dawning of consent. The Labour Party is committed to working actively to building that consent."

By 26 September 1992 Spring appeared to have had a re-think on Articles 2 and 3. In an article in *The Irish Times* he said the creation of conditions for change was vital.

"The right of change in relation to Articles 2 and 3 of our Constitution is vested in the people, and must, by definition, involve the assent of the people," he wrote. "That assent can be willingly given, in the right set of conditions, but those conditions must be put in place. No one has the right to bargain with the Constitution, or to urge that it be given away."

But, significantly, Spring added that there was something equally unreal about those who argued that the Articles could only be on the table if the Government of Ireland Act was on the table too (a position adopted by the FF/Lab Government in 1993).

"Put simply," he wrote, " that's a bit like two men sitting on the roof of a tall building whose ownership they dispute. One man says to the other: 'We can resolve this dispute about ownership if I jump off the building – but I'm prepared to jump if you jump too'."

Once elected Tánaiste and Minister for Foreign Affairs in January 1993, Spring wasted no time in expressing his views on openness towards the North. The new Government would show "openness and flexibility" in any new inter-party talks, he promised, and added that he wanted such talks to take place as a matter of urgency.

While the SDLP welcomed the Government's commitment, Spring's appointment was greeted with scepticism by the

Northern Unionists, notably by Sammy Wilson of the DUP, who dismissed him as a republican from the most republican part of the Republic.

But the SDLP chairman, Mark Durkan, said he was very pleased with Dick Spring's appointment, and with the Northern Ireland section of the Programme for Government.

On 22 January Dick Spring had his first meeting with the Northern Ireland Secretary, Sir Patrick Mayhew. The meeting took place at the Department of Foreign Affairs in Dublin, and afterwards a spokesman said the "personal chemistry was excellent".

The two men met privately for half an hour, after which there was a 90-minute session involving five representatives from both sides.

Spring quickly established a good relationship with the Northern Ireland Secretary and it soon became clear that Sir Patrick saw in Spring hope for attempting yet another initiative on the North.

In an interview with the BBC, Spring said Articles 2 and 3 were not "cast in bronze", a comment which set a new tone in the attitude of the Government.

However, the comments quickly caused concern among Fianna Fáil back-benchers, and one former Minister, West Limerick Deputy Michael J Noonan, was openly critical of the Taoiseach. He subsequently lost the party whip for his critical comments.

Dick Spring's Mansion House speech of 5 March did not propose any new initiative. The Tánaiste covered much of the old ground, but again set a new tone of openness on his part.

He repeated that Articles 2 and 3 "should not remain as if cast in bronze, incapable of change".

"We cannot approach change to our Constitution casually or lightly," he continued. "The issues go far too deep for that.

However, the Constitution was never intended to be an obstacle to mutual understanding on this island and our people would never wish it to be so. If in a new situation there is need – as I expect there will be – of a changed approach to reflect and buttress a new level of mutual understanding, I believe our people will readily be persuaded to endorse change, provided they are satisfied that it does truly serve that purpose."

Spring told the British/Irish Association that the possibility of a united Ireland was a "horizon of fear for the Unionist community", a possibility, as they saw it, of almost unlimited menace to them.

He emphasised that all strands of nationalism agreed that the Unionist community must be seen as partners. What was at issue was how that relationship could be offered on terms the Unionists could accept.

Again he appealed to the Unionists to re-enter inter-Party talks in a new spirit of co-operation.

However, while Dick Spring chose his words well, the political realities on the ground dictated that there would be no movement until at least the aftermath of the local elections in the North in May.

Furthermore, the SDLP Leader, John Hume's decision to enter talks with Sinn Féin sent a further wave of revulsion throughout the Unionist community, who latched onto it as yet another excuse to delay the day of again having to sit around the table with representatives of the Dublin Government.

Meanwhile, the Northern Ireland Secretary, Sir Patrick Mayhew, gave strong indications that the British Government was preparing yet another initiative aimed at a breakthrough. Under the terms of the Anglo-Irish Agreement, the Irish Government felt secure that they would be consulted.

Meanwhile, Tánaiste Dick Spring was experiencing some

embarrassment with some of his back-benchers, notably former Independent Socialist Declan Bree from Sligo.

A strong Republican, Bree had delivered a number of anti-British speeches in the early days of the new Government.

Speaking during a one-day Dáil debate on the North on 1 April, he again attacked British intransigence as the root cause of the troubles in the North of Ireland.

"Day in, day out, week in, week out, year in, year out, the British Tory administration perverts justice by imposing policies that are only appropriate to a totalitarian state," he said. "This is a matter of public record."

The speech caused outrage among the ranks of the Labour Parliamentary Party.

Spring reacted by summoning Deputy Bree to a private meeting, after which he said the deputy had agreed not to undermine him in the future. However, two weeks later, on the eve of a visit to Dublin by British Foreign Secretary Douglas Hurd, Bree spoke in Galway where he accused successive Tory Governments of perverting the course of justice in the North. This time many Labour deputies were openly furious, with some privately saying the party whip should be withdrawn from Bree.

On the morning of Wednesday, 12 May, Spring had another short private meeting with Bree after which he put a motion to the Parliamentary Party which stipulated that all speeches on the North by Deputies should go through the Leader's office.

But Bree still appeared to be undeterred.

On 6 August, while Dick Spring was on holiday in the US, Bree again made a scathing attack on British rule in the North. Speaking in Sligo, on radio station NWR, he said the seeds of the on-going crisis were directly Britain's responsibility.

He refused to accept that he was breaking any agreement with Spring by airing his views on the North.

In his Leader's address to the 1993 Annual Conference in Waterford, Dick Spring devoted six of his 23-page script to Northern Ireland.

He told the delegates he had sought the job of Minister for Foreign Affairs primarily because of his conviction that "Northern Ireland overshadows everything".

"The economic past and future of this island, North and South; the quality of life of the whole island; our ability to develop the kind of services that our people need and deserve – all of these issues are bound up inextricably with the tragedy of Northern Ireland," he said.

As Minister for Foreign Affairs he said he had devoted at least part of every day studying and discussing the complex and painful issues involved.

He again underpinned the importance of the Anglo-Irish Agreement but stressed the Labour Party's "orientation" towards the future.

"Let us talk," he concluded, "without threat, without precondition, without duress. Let us ease the pain of those who are suffering, and do what we can to prevent future suffering. Let us not be found wanting in our time. There is no greater challenge facing us than the challenge of peace, accompanied by reconstruction. And there is no greater opportunity, for all the people of Ireland."

But as time passed, it became obvious that there was a clear divergence of thinking between the Northern Ireland Office and Dublin on the way forward. As the British Prime Minister struggled for his own survival, the likelihood of any real initiative began to fade.

Then in June Anglo-Irish relations were dealt a severe shock when President Robinson sought, and won, Cabinet approval for a visit to West Belfast. Her planned itinerary made it inevitable that she would meet the Sinn Féin leader, Gerry Adams.

The idea sent shock waves through London where the British Prime Minister personally expressed his concern to the Taoiseach during a bilateral meeting in London.

The British Government took such serious exception to the visit that a formal note was delivered to the Irish Government requesting its cancellation on both security and political grounds.

While Albert Reynolds was content to keep a distance, and merely note the concerns with President Robinson, Dick Spring was far more incensed. As far as Spring was concerned, this was a clear breach of the successive Government policy of not meeting any member of Sinn Féin. He greatly feared the knock-on effect on the prospect of talks.

Relations between the President and the Tánaiste were not good since her election in 1990, and many foresaw a real clash. In the days before her visit to Belfast on17 June, Spring visited Áras an Uachtaráin twice to try to dissuade the President from coming into contact with Gerry Adams. However, President Robinson was insistent and, faced with the sole option of cancelling the trip – a number of Labour Ministers were demanding a special Cabinet meeting – the Tánaiste and the Government backed down.

However, just one southern politician, Fine Gael MEP Paddy Cooney, publicly criticised the President's decision to proceed.

The President went ahead with the visit and shook hands with Mr Adams, albeit behind closed doors. But the incident soured relations between the Tánaiste and the President. In effect, she had put it up to the Government, and won. Again she had clearly driven a coach and four through the traditional conception of the Presidency. The confrontation was interpreted by many as a foreshadow of an inevitable showdown with the Government in the future.

But in many ways, Spring's behaviour was rather odd. He

had earlier welcomed the findings of the Opsahl Commission which urged dialogue with Sinn Féin, and he had not condemned a new round of talks between the SDLP leader, John Hume and Mr Adams.

By now, as the deadlock on a future talks continued, Spring decided to take the initiative. In a surprise interview with John Palmer, the Brussels correspondent of *The Guardian*, he announced his belief that the British and Irish Governments might have to seize the initiative and draw up a framework, independent of the parties in the North.

The timing of the publication on 8 July, just days before the traditional 12 July celebrations, raised eyebrows on both sides of the Irish Sea.

In the interview, Spring claimed that the inability of the Northern politicians to get round the negotiating table could not be allowed to paralyse attempts to find a political solution. The two Governments, he said, must take over responsibility for working out a framework.

"We, the Governments, do have some responsibility," he said. "There are many issues where the two Governments have more scope for initiative and more room for manoeuvre than any of the Northern parties, and perhaps it is time to recognise this more clearly."

Spring also hinted at the idea of a supra-national authority for Northern Ireland in which the EC might also be represented. "Something much bigger than our two islands is happening in Europe," he declared.

Ultimately, Spring said an agreement might have to be put directly to the people.

The interview plunged Anglo-Irish relations to a new low.

Already the British Government had rubbished leaked British Labour Party proposals for joint sovereignty put forward in a paper by Kevin McNamara.

British Prime Minister John Major left no doubts where he stood. Speaking in the House of Commons he said the "Union is vital for all parts of the United Kingdom," and that the "Conservative and Unionist Party stands four-square behind it."

In the North, the reaction from Unionist politicians was, as expected, hostile.

DUP councillor, Sammy Wilson, branded Spring a "fascist". He should be called "Dick Tator" rather than Dick Spring, he said.

"Coming from that well-known IRA stronghold in Kerry, Mr Spring's remarks are not surprising and, given his part in the imposition of the Anglo-Irish Agreement, Mr Spring is being a consistent fascist," added Councillor Wilson.

On the day *The Guardian* interview appeared, Spring attended a meeting of the Anglo-Irish Conference in London. Much of it was dominated by the interview.

Later at a press conference, Sir Patrick Mayhew did not hide his anger:

"To be frank, I was surprised by the interview...because that did seem to me to go, in some respects, significantly beyond what I had understood to be the position of the Irish Government... and I thought it did go beyond the cardinal principle, that constitutional principle, that constitutional matters in particular would have to be the subject of agreement across the community if they were to have any prospect of success."

But the meeting did agree on a joint communiqué which declared that "both Governments continue to believe that the objectives of the process remain valid and achievable."

The repercussions continued, however.

Queen's University historian ATQ Stewart expressed the frustrations of the Northern Protestants:

"Dick Spring is out to infuriate and destabilise the Protestants and make them feel powerless in the face of events. But, in fact, he is miscalculating their resolve. Up to now, the loyalists have not had the fertilizer or the timers or the expertise. But they'll get it, and then it will be like Bosnia all over again. I always knew the Anglo-Irish Agreement would end in men with guns in their hands. I see a black cloud ahead."

Writing in the *Sunday Independent*, John A Murphy, Emeritus Professor of History at UCC, said that if there was Unionist anger at the Tánaiste's statements, there was also confusion about the Government's Northern policy.

"Mr Spring," he added, "might well begin by sorting himself out by re-reading the progressive views he expressed little more than a year ago. It is clear that he then regarded the territorial claim as offensive nonsense, and that he thought it was the Republic's business not to pursue the pernicious chimera of unity, or intermediate stages thereof."

Peace enforcing in Somalia would be a "picnic" compared to joint sovereignty in the North, argued Professor Murphy.

"Joint authority would more likely be joint anarchy, and an unsustainable financial and security burden on the Republic."

Former Coalition Minister John Boland warned that Spring's "tight-rope" behaviour could force an embattled John Major into a policy of appeasement with the Unionists.

It happened on Thursday, 22 July, when the British Government secured the agreement of the nine Ulster Unionist MPs to support them in a vote against a Labour amendment supporting the Social Chapter of the Maastricht Treaty. The move helped save John Major from acute embarrassment, but made him vulnerable with the Unionists.

As rumours of a deal with the Unionists spread throughout the House of Commons, Dick Spring got on the phone to Sir Patrick Mayhew. John Major moved to ease the tension by stating "nothing was asked for, nothing was offered, and nothing was given." But no serious Southern politician believed him.

In September, it was revealed that Dick Spring had discussed the idea of a US envoy to the North, when he met former President, Jimmy Carter, at a Human Rights Convention in Vienna earlier in the summer. The idea of an envoy had been suggested by President Clinton during his presidential election campaign.

The Government played down the significance of the Carter/Spring meeting, but confirmed that the notion of a US envoy was one "option" that would be considered in the event of the failure of inter-party talks to re-commence.

Then on 25 September, SDLP leader John Hume and Sinn Féin President Gerry Adams unexpectedly announced that they had prepared a "report" for the Irish Government. In the meantime their talks had been "suspended".

23
A SOUND MAN?

Standing on the podium at the 1993 Annual Conference in Jury's Hotel, Waterford, Dick Spring could reflect on a very impressive achievement.

Now just 80 days in office there was already a lot to report.

Two years previously, in Killarney, he had set the objective of becoming the second largest political party. Now he could joke that the delegates thought he expected them to make the breakthrough on the very first attempt.

Labour was now represented in nearly every county in Ireland from Donegal to Kerry. Everywhere you looked Labour was on the map, and on the march.

The change was impressive.

Take Co Monaghan, for example. Prior to the general election there was just one registered member of the Labour Party in the county, young solicitor Ann Gallagher, who was herself a native of County Leitrim. From a Fine Gael background, she had joined the party while studying in Trinity College. There were just ten members in neighbouring Cavan.

In the November 1992 general election she had almost made it to the Dáil in one of the most dramatic breakthroughs ever for the party. She was later elected to the Seanad, and today there are six branches of the party in Cavan/Monaghan with over 100 members.

The party had also secured a respectable representation of women, with five members either deputies or senators, three of them holding Ministerial office.

Proudly, Dick Spring could boast that the country's oldest political party was now the major force in Irish politics.

Spring rightly admitted that he had hesitated before going into Government with Fianna Fáil, but he said he had no regrets. He admitted, too, that they had made some mistakes, notably in the appointment of advisers.

Spring referred to nineteenth century novelist Jules Verne, a writer who had popularised the idea of change in the future for millions of readers. He had written about landing on the moon before aircraft were invented, and about new methods of travel and discovery.

"His most famous book, *Around the World in Eighty Days,*" said Spring, "is a stirring tale of an impossible journey successfully accomplished. Well, tonight, oddly enough, the Labour Party has just completed 'In Government for Eighty Days' – and there are lots of stirring tales yet to be told!"

The Government was finally beginning to enjoy something akin to a honeymoon period, but the advisers fiasco had left a bad taste.

The early days of the Government had seen a number of obstacles, not least of which was the currency crisis. Despite repeated pleas, the EC failed to move to protect the punt, and having stubbornly held out for some weeks, the Government was finally forced to devalue by 10 per cent.

It was a red-faced Dick Spring who, in early February, berated his European counterparts for not giving support at the first ever televised meeting of EC Foreign Ministers.

"Unless we act together we could be picked off one by one," he told reporters in Brussels.

The currency crisis solved, and interests rates tumbling down, the Government was soon faced with the embarrassing sale of the State's stake in Greencore, formerly the Irish Sugar Company.

An attempt by American food giant ADM to buy the company was stymied when Labour back-benchers, led by Dublin South-Central Deputy Pat Upton, objected.

ADM lost interest and the Government was left with egg on its face when stockbrokers J & E Davy were unable to dispose of all the shares to financial institutions and ended up selling a sizeable portion to four of their own holding companies.

The débâcle raised questions about how successfully the new concept of partnership Government was working.

Deputy Pat Rabbitte, rated one of the top Dáil performers, argues that Dick Spring was too quick to respond to Pat Upton's comments, "which I think were not any more seriously held than to keep Pat Upton with some kind of profile".

Rabbitte says it yet remains to be seen how effective the entire experiment of the office of Tánaiste is.

"I would say the Greencore sale was one very negative example. It would appear that the Tánaiste, acting at the behest of the back-benchers, was successful in stopping the sale of the shares to ADM. However, what materialised was the sale of the shares in any event resulting in a worse position than lining in with a major international company which had access to international markets and could bring in resources for the capitalisation and expansion of Greencore.

"My own view was that the State ought to have retained that shareholding as a means of exerting strategic influence in the development of a major indigenous company. But the position the Minister for Finance, Bertie Ahern, was pushed into, was neither one thing nor the other. If the effect of the Tánaiste's office is to merely act as a spoiler, I don't think that anybody is going to be the beneficiary in the long term."

As 1993 wore on, events led to a straining of relations within the partnership.

A report in a British newspaper in May that Cable and Wireless was interested in buying a stake in Telecom Éireann caused Spring to announce that the Labour Party would leave Government rather than allow such a development.

This was followed later the same week by the Taoiseach, against the advice of many Labour Ministers and his own Finance Minister, ramming a tax amnesty through the Cabinet.

The idea of an amnesty for tax cheats was regarded as "part of the Fianna Fáil agenda" and Labour advisers openly said they would not promote the concept.

"It is not the thing that the Labour Party in Government should be doing," said Dublin Central Deputy, Joe Costello. "It gives out all the wrong signals."

But every Labour deputy supported the amnesty in the Dáil vote.

Then came the Aer Lingus plan, yet another major crisis for the Labour deputies, particularly those new Members on Dublin's northside.

Again, following a series of meetings and briefings by Transport Minister Brian Cowen, all the Labour deputies supported the Government in a Dáil vote on a rescue plan during Private Members' Time. Ironically, two Fianna Fáil deputies in Clare, resigned the party whip because of perceived negative implications for Shannon.

In September the situation became more tense when only 700 of the required 1,280 Aer Lingus staff volunteered for redundancy. Labour deputies had insisted there would be no forced redundancies.

Finally, in June it fell to the lot of Dick Spring to negotiate Ireland's £8 billion in EC Structural Funds, a figure which the Taoiseach had claimed to have "in the bag" since the Edinburgh Summit in December 1992. The promise of this money had been critical in securing Labour's support for Coalition. Commentators referred to the money as "the dowry" for the marriage of the two parties.

Spring had invested his credibility as much as Albert Reynolds had in securing the money. In the end he secured £7.84 billion, enough to save face, and a potential crisis was averted.

So how will history view Dick Spring?

His early period in Government in the 1983-87 Coalition shows him as a competent, but lack-lustre performer.

He left no lasting mark as Minister of State for Justice in 1981, or as Minister for the Environment and Energy. That period is best remembered for the terrible infighting and ideological divisions within the Labour party. The instability partly helped to pave the way for the emergence of the Progressive Democrats.

But it was in Opposition, and in getting a firm grip on the leadership of the Labour Party, that he excelled.

He will be seen as someone who, from a position of great weakness initially, managed to get control of the Labour Party like no other leader did, and who brought back 33 deputies, which was an unprecedented high in the party's history. These were no mean achievements.

Says Pat Rabbitte: "In Opposition he has shown himself to have characteristics and ruthlessness which I think are necessary in a serious politician. His no-holds barred confrontation with Charles Haughey marked him out as someone who is not afraid to push the boat out, and he did prove himself ruthless."

The Labour Party's success, against the odds, in putting Mary Robinson in the Phoenix Park, crowned his position as the leader of the Opposition in the Dáil and firmly put him in the front line of politics.

In July 1989, he pulled off a major coup when he questioned Charles Haughey's plan to remain on as Taoiseach when he could not form a Government. Haughey was eventually forced to accept Spring's view and resign to become acting Taoiseach.

Again he out-manoeuvered Fine Gael when he told the Dáil that Mr Haughey did not intend to re-appoint Michael Mills as Ombudsman. The ensuing controversy resulted in Mills keeping his job.

But probably his best Dáil performance was his contribution on the Goodman affair when the Dáil was recalled in August 1990, to amend the Companies Bill. The Fine Gael Leader, Alan Dukes, had been embarrassed when it was revealed that bankers had given inside information to Spring, rather than to Fine Gael, fearing they would not use it effectively. Spring had come a long way from that dreadful time back at the Party's Annual Conference in Cork in 1987 when he lost his temper and shouted: "I'm not taking this any more!"

But Spring now faces the test of being as good in office as he had been in Opposition.

The history of Coalition Governments in the Republic has been that the smaller party invariably suffers.

"Labour is up against it," says Pat Rabbitte, "if they are not seen to be able to put 100,000 people back to work. That's what really matters at the end of the day. It is the issue that will determine whether they grow or not at the next election."

Spring has also pulled the party to the Right, and broadened its appeal to the Irish electorate.

"I don't think he is a very ideological leader of the Labour Party," says Rabbitte. "I think you will search very far in any of his set speeches to find any reference to the word 'socialism.' His addresses to the party conferences have always been noteworthy for their absence of any expressed reference of any socialist convictions. In that he has been fortunate in having been able to trim his sails and accommodate himself to the middle ground. That has electorally benefited him, but he has also pulled the Labour Party to the Right."

Former Cabinet colleague Alan Dukes is quite critical.

Spring, he says, can be proud of the part he played in bringing about the Anglo-Irish Agreement, but the inspiration and persuasion were Garret FitzGerald's.

"It was no statesman who described Charles Haughey as the virus causing a virus in the body politic, and then, when Haughey was deposed, said it was too early to assess the man's contribution to Irish politics, and more recently said he had a 'touch of class'.

"Reading the pretentiously titled 'Programme for a Partnership Government' which emerged from lengthy negotiations based on a Fianna Fáil document, I ask: What has changed?"

Another Cabinet colleague, John Boland, notes Spring's "amazing acrobatic display upon the highest and most public of ropes" in entering Government with his previously sworn enemies. Yet he emerged with a disciplined party.

And what of the future?

His greatest test, no doubt, will be on Northern Ireland.

The ground is littered with dangers.

According to John Boland, it is one thing to dabble in the political futures of the denizens of Leinster House, quite another when your actions may either help to precipitate the downfall of Major's Government or, alternatively, drive it into adopting a policy of appeasement, if not outright rapprochement, with the Unionists.

"Mr Spring should consider carefully before he ventures further on this particular wire. It could be a long fall for all of us from way out there. And there is no safety net."

Maurice Manning believes that, to date, Dick Spring's influence on the North has been negative.

"He has very consciously adopted a fairly hardline green stance. I think he has undone much of the good work done to convince the Unionists of the goodwill of the Southern Government. When

Fianna Fáil and the Progressive Democrats were in power, the Unionists could at least expect their point of view to have been understood by the PDs. They looked to Labour, and in particular to Dick Spring, for a similar input. Up to now what they've got is two parties vying with each other to prove which is the more macho on the green issue."

Former Labour Leader Michael O'Leary believes Dick Spring's major contribution to Irish political life will be on Northern Ireland.

"This is the first time that Labour has had that role and Spring will use it. He will certainly make an impact on this question.

"I don't think anyone has a magic wand, but he gives confidence. It's inevitable that Labour will grow. I see Dick Spring as Taoiseach, possibly as soon as the next Dáil."

Nor would Pat Rabbitte rule Spring out as a future Taoiseach in a majority Government. But he warns that the allegiance of some of the middle class supporters is very thin and they can desert the ship very easily.

"Overall," he says, "Spring has not been a conviction politician, but he has been a good performer."

Former Fianna Fáil Minister Neil Blaney is impressed by Spring.

"I rate him. Two and half years ago, I rated him nowhere," he said in an interview with the *Sunday Business Post* in August 1993. "Then he began to come through in the Parliament. I was confused about his poor profile up to that point and his improved performance since then. I'm satisfied that it was Fergus Finlay and John Rogers, two people whom he met every Wednesday the sun shone, who made him and them a good team."

But, added Blaney: "He did make a few blunders early on. He was almost indicating that Articles 2 and 3 were available but he pulled back from that. Maybe it was the advice he got from his backroom people. Or his people in Kerry; they probably straightened him out there."

In Maurice Manning's view, Spring will go down as one of the most significant Irish politicians of the twentieth century.

"First of all he has captured the public imagination in a way that very few have this century – Collins, de Valera, Garret FitzGerald, Charlie Haughey, Dick Spring. All of them in their own way have captured the public imagination and are equated in the public mind with major changes. He has certainly lifted and transformed the Labour Party into a disciplined and cohesive party. In the process he has drained that party of much of what gave it its meaning for Irish people, and much of what it stood for originally. He has drained it of much of its ideological sustenance. Clearly it's too early to see whether the monument he has created will endure. But certainly he has made an impact greater than any Labour Party leader to this date."

In the meantime, the gale force winds are still out there, and they may return with increased vigour on such issues as the rescue of Aer Lingus, the proposed White Paper on education, and most of all, the Northern Ireland question. An IMS poll in September showed Labour already slipping in the polls with a 16 per cent rating, compared to 19 per cent in the November election.

But how would Dick Spring, himself, like to be remembered?

There is a story that Dick Spring tells about a letter he received from fellow Kerryman Brendan Kennelly on the death of his father.

Kennelly wrote that he had been in Kerry at election time when Dan Spring was out campaigning. The poet's sleeve was pulled by an old fellow who advised him to give his first preference to Spring senior.

"He's the one to vote for. He's a sound man," said the old fellow.

It's probably the kind of thing that Dick Spring would like to have said about himself.

Bibliography

Browne, Vincent (Ed) *The Magill Book of Irish Politics*, Magill Publications 1981.

Browne, Vincent (Ed) *The Magill Guide to Election '82*, Magill Publications 1982.

Cooney, John *The Crozier and the Dáil: Church and State in Ireland 1922 - 1986*, Mercier Press, 1986.

Farrell, Michael (Ed) *Magill Book of Irish Politics 1984*, Magill Publications, 1983.

Finley, Fergus *Mary Robinson, A President with a Purpose*, O'Brien Press, 1990.

FitzGerald, Garret *All in a Life, an Autobiography*, Gill and Macmillan 1991.

Gallagher, Michael *The Irish Labour Party in Transition 1957 - 1982*, University Press, 1982.

Gallagher, Michael *Political Parties in the Republic*, Gill and Macmillan, 1985.

Horgan, John *Labour: The Price of Power*, Gill and Macmillan 1986.

Hussey, Gemma, *At the Cutting Edge, Cabinet Diaries 1982 - 1987*, Gill and Macmillan 1990.

O'Beirnes, Stephen *Hiding Behind a Face, Fine Gael Under FitzGerald*, Gill and Macmillan, 1986.

O'Reilly, Emily *Candidate*, Attic Press, 1991.

O'Sullivan, Michael *Mary Robinson: The Life and Times of an Irish Liberal*, Blackwater Press, 1993.

Rafter, Kevin and Whelan, Noel *From Malin Head to Mizen Head, The Definitive Guide to Local Government in Ireland*, Blackwater Press 1992.

Ryan, Tim *Mara, P.J.*, Blackwater Press 1992.

Trench, Brian (Ed). *Election '87*, Magill Publications 1987.

Index